For Teachers Only

For Teachers Only

A Lesson Plan for Life . . .

Demarcus Devon Copeland

BOOKLOGIX®
Alpharetta, GA

ISBN: 978-1-6653-0391-0 - Paperback
eISBN: 978-1-6653-0392-7 - eBook

Library of Congress Control Number: 2022908400

♾This paper meets the requirements of ANSI/NISO Z39.48-1992 (Permanence of Paper)

0 5 2 6 2 2

To all those who planted and the ones that watered, and to God, who gives the increase.

CONTENTS

FOREWORD

My future career choice was sealed in second grade. It wasn't because my teacher taught a unit on occupations, but it was something she taught me . . . however inadvertently. She was young. And she was pretty. And she was nice. But she was not a very good teacher. Consequently, I was zipping through my school year not learning a thing—and having a great time—until my report card came out and my math grade was really low.

So, my dad stepped in to help me with homework. I was clueless. He taught me how to work the problems, and the next day in class I was the only volunteer to raise my hand to answer the first homework question. I was asked to come to the board and explain how I did it. As I did so, I felt confident and smart! I was eager for my next lesson with Dad that night.

So, it continued. My dad taught me, and I taught my class. And it was then that I set my sails for a teaching career and would not be dissuaded (even when my dad pressed me hard to be a math major). I entered my first classroom like most teachers: with great expectations of myself and my students. I would change the world one classroom at a time. That was the year I finally gained compassion for my second-grade teacher.

Bit by bit, the challenges of teaching drained away my confidence and the twinkle in my eye when I thought about teaching. Midway through my teaching journey, I had the privilege of being in the classroom with Mr. D. C. When I first read this book, I had no doubt that I was "fodder" for some of his writing. Sometimes I was a good example, but sadly, many times I fell short. Over our five-year history in a psychoeducational setting of planning lessons, scrapping them to deal with problem behaviors, thriving one minute (barely surviving the next), and always debriefing at day's end, we learned and grew.

This book was conceived and brought forth by a man who is dedicated to teaching and is passionate about his students. It will shine a spotlight to help us all stay reminded of the why and how of this demanding profession. It will stir up the gift of true teaching. It will separate the wheat from the chaff in daily-life terms. Absorb it and be renewed and refreshed! Digest it and carry on!

—Susan Rutherford
Special-Education Teacher

INTRODUCTION

I wish I could tell you that it's going to get better; just wait. I wish I could tell you society was on your side. I wish I could give you all $1 million in retirement each, but unfortunately, that would not be the truth. The truth is, the realities of your circumstances are dire. Your workload continues to increase, the kids are less interested in learning and more interested in making a statement, and the job itself is of no interest in making any of this better for you in the near future. It is not because the government, superintendent, or even your principal lacks interest in helping—they just don't know how to help you best.

So, this leads you to do what you can to help yourself: You buy books and take classes, trying to increase your chances of making more money. You make an attempt to create some sort of balance in your life, which begins to provoke your chances of burnout. You push and push and push until you have nothing left to give, and you become numb and powerless to make a difference. You were like a potted flower meant to stand out and be beautiful—your color made to be vibrant, your purpose manifested in the most subtle way, and your harvest everlasting. The sun was always supposed to shine on you and water always made available to you. And because you never intended to be moved, you blossomed where you were planted. But somewhere along the way someone closed the window and shielded the sunlight, and forgot you were still there. I am deeply sorry that it has taken me so long to bring this book to you, but I'm happy it's finally here.

Hello, my name is Mr. D. C.—or more formally known as Demarcus Devon Copeland—and I am a certified life coach for teachers and students. I have created two things in conjunction with my calling: M-PACK, for the students, and this book, for the teachers.

I have devoted the youthful portion of my life to helping others in as many ways as possible, more specifically in youth-related projects. Over the course of ten years I have tried to lose myself in the act of serving others. I've served as a youth minister, youth-development specialist, recreation coach, life coach, leadership coach, after-school certified tutor, and a special-education paraprofessional. Being inside a school system opened my eyes to many things and enhanced my ability to communicate and connect with youth.

After a period of deep introspective thinking, I decided, given my time spent with students and teachers (which was well over ten thousand hours), I was ready to transition deeper in my calling. I began by creating a nonprofit organization that focused on providing life-coaching services to students who faced adverse childhood experiences called "Molding Passionate Active Creative Kids Corporation" (M-PACK). M-PACK allowed me to personally grasp the needs of students coming from a dysfunctional setting in the hopes of reaching one to gain the other.

While observing youth, I couldn't help but to learn what makes them tick. I paid close attention to how they were responding in an effort to ascertain what to do and what not to do to reach them. Yet the one thing that stood out was not so much what they did as it was how I was responding to them. Most of the time I was responding emotionally, other times emotionlessly. Sometimes I was very stern, while other times easygoing. However, in every setting, stress was shaping the way I was communicating with the students. This is what intrigued me; I was becoming more interested in how the students and I were responding to one another and what I needed to do to get in harmony with them. It reshaped my mode of thinking, broadening my perception to a more calculated approach. I realized it had less to do with the students—it was I that was the primary factor shaping the interactions!

I continued my research through my efforts with M-PACK, but I also began studying teachers and paying close attention to how they were feeling. I often recognized that health issues, lack of energy, and difficulty in the home were factors affecting their work ethic. It broke my heart. They were trying to make a difference, but they just didn't have anything left to give. This motivated me to find a way to contribute to making their lives easier. My efforts only helped a day at a time, and it also depended on the teacher I was helping. I had no long-term antidote available . . . yet!

The news has recently reported a mass exodus of teachers from the profession. This is a major issue. With numbers of students per class, paper workload, and cost of living all going up at the same time, teachers are feeling overworked and unappreciated, not including the cultural transformation of youth across the world. Society is a constant influence with music and social media drowning out the voices of our teachers. It makes for a discouraging and often dangerous environment—literally! Even when our teachers think they are beginning to get ahead, things change. It's like running from a lion only to run into a bear, and finally escaping the bear only to be bitten by a snake. Teachers have had enough. Public education is having an overall negative effect on its victims, leaving them in a helpless situation.

Yet history proves that the most dire situations are the ripest for a hero to emerge. As a paraprofessional for the GNETs program and other therapeutic education systems, I have had the pleasure of working with many underprivileged students who come from many different backgrounds, and unfortunately, some of those places were horrific. These classrooms have brought me into shared environments with physically, emotionally, and sexually abused children. My concern is that we may be looking ahead to dark days if we do not get involved sooner.

People are looking for all kinds of ways to make the school system better for its students. Money is added to the budget, speakers are brought in, and the standards are constantly changing to better suit the students' needs. Nevertheless, public education is slowly losing its worth to students, teachers, and parents. In spite of all this, I believe there are ways to fix the current situation, but the most effective place to start is with the teachers.

I believe my book is an excellent way to start out the school year or the new year if you are currently in the field of education. To my knowledge, our education department has backed teachers into a corner that is challenging to escape. Our current culture presents many hurdles to jump in order to pay the bills, have time for family, and keep up with personal responsibilities. It is difficult to find balance. This book was written to help you cultivate balance in your life as an educator.

I believe I have found the answer to burnout—well, a tool that could prevent burnout. I believe there are three primary steps that we must take to better connect with the students, and it starts with us. This book focuses on what you need from you, what the school needs from you, and what the students need from you. It may seem second nature at first, but the students have to come last in this situation. As you move through this book, you will better understand why that must be the case.

For some, this book may be the beginning of a new life; for others, just a tool to maintain your life, but . . . *this is for teachers only*! I leave you with a quote that used to be posted in the teacher's restroom of a school I worked at:

> I've come to the frightening conclusion that I am the decisive element in the classroom. It's my daily mood that makes the weather. As a teacher, I possess a tremendous power to make a child's life miserable or joyous. I can be a tool of torture or an instrument of inspiration. I can humiliate or humor, hurt or heal. In all situations, it is my response that decides whether a crisis will be escalated or de-escalated and a child humanized or dehumanized.
>
> —Dr. Haim Ginott

Part 1

What You Need from You . . .

Self-Care

In a book I read some time ago called *Love Is Letting Go of Fear* by Gerald G. Jampolsky, MD, it states, in the simplest way, these words:

> Peace of mind as our single goal is the most potent motivating force we can have. To have inner peace we need to be consistent in having peace of mind as our single goal. We are all tempted to try and juggle multiple goals. Juggling can only serve to deflect our focus and increase our conflict. We can achieve consistency in keeping this single goal in mind by reminding ourselves of the singleness of purpose we would have if we suddenly found ourselves drowning in the ocean. We would, in that situation, put all of our attention into the single goal of staying afloat and breathing for survival.

How many of us really take self-care seriously? Self-care is defined as "practicing and taking action to preserve or improve one's health."[1] Not only are educators missing the benefits of it; other workers are, too. How many of us have spent our lives

[1] https://uwaterloo.ca/thrive-tookit/what-self-care-and-why-it-important.

chasing a clock and a paycheck, and at the end of each day we have nothing in return for ourselves? I can remember days spent in a classroom not feeling all that great about the job I was doing and thinking no one genuinely cared. I went to my job with the world on my shoulders, hoping—or better yet, expecting—someone to ask if I was okay, but my job did not provide that type of self-care.

At the end of the day, my mental state depended on how the day had gone at school. Most days, this was not a good place. I began to dread waking up in the morning to go to my job. I even got to the point where I asked myself if I hated my job. I soon found out that hating my job was not the problem; I was just overwhelmed from a lack of self-care. Even if I got the job of my dreams, I would still need time to decompress and maintain my personal interest.

Maintaining your personal interest is how you are going to begin to provide your own self-care or caring about yourself above all else. There are many teachers walking into their classroom day in and day out believing that the children were the only ones who were at risk. Sadly, if this is you, you have been mistaken, because it is also you who are at risk.

Many teachers are at risk of losing the simple joys that come with working with children. What I am referring to are the things that no amount of money could buy and that which you will never learn in college, possibilities that are irreplaceable and noncontestant: the love—the pure, refined love—that surpasses all understanding, the love for other people's children. And as a result, you begin to become someone that you never intended to be, with or without the classroom. You begin to become someone that does not like children, and it has nothing to do with them and everything to do with you.

A day in the life of a teacher is extremely demanding. From the time you get out of bed in the morning, your job is to serve others. For many of us, it is our responsibility to gather all that is needed to start the day—things like taking the pets out, washing leftover dishes, cooking breakfast, and getting children ready for school. Your shift starts before anyone else's because it starts at home. You wake up to see the day ahead of you, and it is sometimes enough to make you feel like quitting. Most days, it feels like a series of chores. But you get it done.

I work with a single mother who is also an educator, and every day before she arrives at school she has to feed and prepare herself and her daughter for the day. She tells me she has to wake up three hours before work just to get everything done on time. Most days, she arrives at work before I do, and I have no children to excuse my tardiness. Though we both go into the same job, unlike her I only have the students in my classroom to worry about. She has students and a child of her own.

When she enters her classroom, she might find leftover work from the day before, such as lesson plans or printing or copying materials. As her students arrive, she is presented with another challenge because she doesn't know how their morning has been so far. A number of her students may have had a great morning, but others may have not (sleep deprivation, missed breakfast, or them just feeling embarrassed about the way they are dressed). Regardless, it is her job to manage everyone's attitude, including her own. So, the question in her mind is not if she can do it, but how? How as an educator can she become a mental-health coach for herself and her students all at the same time? She will need energy, time, and patience, not to mention a strategy.

Without the right strategy, she may feel obligated to stay at work after school hours. However, she has a daughter she needs to get to gymnastic practice. She quickly finds herself shifting gears from taking care of other people's children to her own, which is when overtime begins. For a single mother, this means she continues to give more of herself beyond the school day.

However, consider a similar scenario with two additional kids, a husband, and a pet. Together with the continued caregiving duties after school, many teachers find themselves with little to no time to decompress.

In my mind, this very situation makes educators superheroes—completely selfless! Even when it's a struggle, they usually find a way to do what they need to do and maintain and more. Although this schedule is unsustainable, it is happening every day. With such a demanding schedule, life, and all that comes with being human, is there time for anyone in education to have time for self-care?

Well, not really, but you and I are going to have to find time to make it happen because it is essential for your effectiveness in working with children. There is a notion that gets passed around in many other professions that you cannot serve others without first serving yourself. For instance, if you were on a plane and the flight attendant asked you to put on your oxygen mask, most mothers would attempt to put masks on their children first. There is nothing inherently wrong with that; it's a mother's instinct. But the flight attendant makes it clear that you should put your mask on first! Believe me, a child can go a few minutes without oxygen and do just fine in life, but how well will that same child do without a mother or a father? Self-care is the oxygen we all need to get the job done. So, how we are going to make time for self-care will be our primary focus.

We all know there are twenty-four hours in a day. You must find the minutes within the hours that work best for you.

Writer Henry David Thoreau wrote, "Many an object is not seen, though it falls within the range of our visual ray, because it does not come within the range of our intellectual ray."

The reason most teachers do not find time for self-care is because they do not see it as important enough to make time for. One of my favorite quotes is "Out of sight, out of mind." If it has not been brought to your attention, chances are you are not thinking about it. Self-neglect becomes a normal thing when surrounded by people who are also neglecting themselves (birds of a feather flock together). While working in the school system, you would not believe the mentality of the teachers that I was surrounded by: low self-esteem, loneliness, and somewhat bitter, all working with the happiest beings in the world—children.

There is a story that comes to mind from the Bible that really brings this point home.

The Healing at the Pool (John 5, NIV)

> *Some time later, Jesus went up to Jerusalem for one of the Jewish festivals. Now there is in Jerusalem near the Sheep Gate a pool, which in Aramaic is called Bethesda and which is surrounded by five covered colonnades. Here a great number of disabled people used to lie—the blind, the lame, the paralyzed. One who was there had been an invalid for thirty-eight years. When Jesus saw him lying there and learned that he had been in this condition for a long time, he asked him, "Do you want to get well?"*
>
> *"Sir," the invalid replied, "I have no one to help me into the pool when the water is stirred. While I am trying to get in, someone else goes down ahead of me."*
>
> *Then Jesus said to him, "Get up! Pick up your mat and walk." At once the man was cured; he picked up his mat and walked.*

What I really want us to take a closer look at is verse 7: "I have no one to help me into the pool when the water is stirred." People who are exactly like you surround you, and you are expecting them to give you advice about how to handle it. The people around the man could not walk, and he was asking them to help him. But what a joy it must have been when this man decided that he did want to be well, so he got up, picked up his mat, and walked out of that place forever.

In the school building, I hear this kind of thing happening too often. Questions circulate like, "What do you do? What do you drink? Who is your weed man?" Yes, that has been said in school buildings. What I find is that these are not ways to self-care. These are escape methods, and it only makes problems worse. Remember at the beginning of the chapter when we were talking about the singleness of goal being a peace of mind? The goal is to heal it, not escape it. It not only leads to burnout, but also many other underlying issues which I will not go into because I'm not a doctor.

But let's just leave it at this: when you run out of time and don't think you will have time to cook, you will pick up the most convenient thing possible. I call this the fast-food method to a better life—when we go trying to get help from anybody anywhere. This may happen multiple times in a week, and we all know it is very unhealthy for you. We can't continue to take advice from everybody.

So, since we know now that it is not easy to have this kind of schedule nor is it healthy, how do we fix it? What do we do? Dr. Caroline Leaf, the author of *The Perfect You*, refers to active self-regulation:

> Conscious cognitive thinking is called active self-regulation. The deeper we think, the more active self-regulation interacts with dynamic self-regulation. Active self-regulation is intentional and controlled by your choice to pay attention to something. Its effectiveness is determined by how mindful and deliberate you are in any given moment.
>
> It is important to remember that thoughts (also known as descriptive systems of memories) are automatized (made into a habit) through a deliberate, repeated, and conscious cognitive thinking. This type of thinking has to occur for a minimum of three cycles of twenty-one days . . . in order for true understanding to take place.

In other words, you must be intentional about who you are and what you want. As Shakespeare puts it, "To thine own self be true." Self-care will become your best friend when you begin to do it the correct way. I say this only because there is an incorrect way of doing it. There are things we all love to do, but some of these things may not be good for our overall health. We must invest into today for a better tomorrow. Great examples of self-care are exercising, taking a hot bath, or a nice walk (anywhere children are not present, because if they are, you might be tempted to go into teacher mode).

Self-care has to be physically put on your calendar, otherwise you will neglect it. Just saying what you would like to do is not enough—make it happen! Start small. Teachers have more time off than any other job in the world. How can you not make time for it? Of all jobs, as an educator you have no excuse. Not only will this one thing improve your productivity in the classroom, but also it will make you happier in your overall life.

Listen, I get it! You may not know exactly how this will work for you, and you're not even sure if you can do this and life at the same time. Well, I honestly don't think you have a choice. Though you are a hero, you are also part human, and that side of you is emotional and, at times, unstable. So, just understand you were not created for the rigor of life to be that demanding and complicated. The only reason you are even able to push yourself that hard is because of how you were formed in the womb of your mother. You are a survivor, no matter what life—or even that job—brings you.

You are more than capable of doing the job well. But the daunting fact that comes to mind is you were made for much more than survival—you were made to thrive! And to be extremely happy doing it. Self-care is all about how you are going to get to that mental place where you are full of positive energy, because at the end of the day, how can you give what even *you* don't possess? Your self-care may be the only thing standing in the way of the energy of your classroom.

I work with kids for twelve hours a day. The first half is special education, and the second half is the after-school program with the bottom 25 percent of students. I have to decompress every day. I do a lot of simple things. I ask myself, *What would I like to eat when I get off?* Even if it is way out of the way to get it, I make sure I do.

Now, of course, if you have children, this may not be as practical for you, but there are other alternatives. As for me, though, this gives me something to look forward to, and it helps me keep in mind that this school is not the whole world. When I leave this place, I can do whatever I want to do.

Self-care is having something to look forward to constantly. Sometimes it's looking forward to having a cup of coffee with a coworker or a date. Whatever you decide to do, make sure it does not affect the next day. As I said, when you leave the school, you can do whatever you want, but it isn't like Vegas—it will surely come with you the next morning.

Questions for Self-Reflection

1. Have you found yourself juggling multiple goals for your class? If so, how can you find a way to seek out one goal that balances out the lot?

____
____
____
____
____

2. What are personal interests of yours that you have been neglecting because of your work schedule?

____
____
____
____
____

3. Does your family interfere with your self-care? Yes or no.

4. How will you intentionally make time for self-care?

____
____
____
____
____

5. List five things you could do for self-care!
   - _______________________________________
   - _______________________________________
   - _______________________________________
   - _______________________________________
   - _______________________________________

MOTIVATION

> Let your rapidity be that of the wind. Your gentleness that of the forest. In raiding and plundering be like fire, be immovable like a mountain. Be as hard to know as the shadow and move as fast as lighting.

This was a video I listened to called "The Warrior's Mindset - *The Art of War* by Sun Tzu." Now it is very important that you do not take me wrong; I find this to be very useful, though you may not be going into a physical battle. It has been said many times over that the real battlefield is in the mind, and the heaviest burden that we carry is our thoughts. If this is the case, then staying motivated needs to be one of our primary focuses.

Motivation is defined as a reason or reasons one has for acting or behaving in a particular way. We all know good and well that working at a school does not provide constant motivation—not the kids, not the money, not the boss. Let us just be real: Most (many) mornings we think about calling out, or we are counting the days until break! Is that not sad? We are more motivated to stay out than go in. I don't know about you, but that alone makes me laugh yet also cringe a little on the inside.

How are we supposed to make a difference in the lives that are sent to us if we are not feeling it ourselves? The better question is, how can you motivate if you are not motivated yourself?

This will have to be a self-exploration. With mental health being a relevant and real issue in this day and age, there is no telling what people will do to self-motivate to regulate.

How many of you have woken up to the sound of an alarm clock and immediately you felt unmotivated to go to work? Just the sound of that electrical device makes your flesh crawl. And it doesn't matter what sound it makes. I've tried putting my favorite song as an alarm, but I'll tell you this, that's quickest way for a song to go from the Billboard Hot 100 to hells bells and out of your music library in a heartbeat. Even the voice of angels could not motivate me to wake up in the morning.

When it comes to getting motivated, your routine in the morning is the key to it all. How your day begins is how your day will end. As it is often said in the church, "Y'all don't hear me." Turn to your neighbor and say, "How your day begins is how your day will end." That has been a true statement for me my entire life, even as a kid, and it is a lesson I had to learn on my own.

I did a horrible job controlling my thought patterns. I used to wake up and say out loud, "I don't want to go to this job," and even before bed I used to say it. "I don't want to go to this job in the morning."

The Bible tells us that the power of life and death is in the tongue. The whole day would be out of whack at that point. No "good mornings," no "hellos," no nothing. But this was when I was working at a pizza restaurant, and the first problem there is I truly did hate my job and should not have been there in the first place.

Now let's take a praise break for a second. Matthew 6:21 (NIV): "For where your treasure is, there your heart will be also." First and foremost, wherever you decide to work, motivation will only come if you like where you are.

My motivation never developed while working at the pizza place, and I worked my way from the sign shaker to the absolute top: running and owning a store. I was looking at making

$150,000 a year at the age of twenty-two. But at the time, I also was working at two schools part time, and my pizza job was asking me to leave the schools and promising I'd get paid for it. I'm not going to lie, I quit one of my jobs because I believed that to be true. And I cried like a baby as I walked away from those kids.

Every day at the pizza place I tried and tried and tried to get motivated about being there, but I just could not. It only took me three months to realize I needed to quit the pizza place completely and work with kids full time. Now, five years later, I'm twenty-six and you are reading a book by me about education. Where your treasure is, there your heart will be also.

If you are in education, you need to question your motivation to stay and whether it is strong enough to keep you. If you do not want to teach, you need to quit while you are ahead because this is not a job for people who feel abused. This is a job for heroes, period. It will be warfare in that classroom each and every day, no matter how you feel about the job, good or bad. That is the art of war in the classroom. If you are not motivated to stay in this profession, then you have nothing to offer children who did not ask for you as a teacher. In the words of a counselor to a student, "Get your life together".

I did what I had to do to get to a place where I wanted to be. And I know that sounds like some generic, overused, motivational rhetoric, but it is true: you have to make the change. I want to be with children in the trenches—me, their general, and them, soldiers—and I'm extremely motivated to stay on this battlefield with them in this profession.

So, let's go back to the beginning: how your day begins is how your day ends. As soon as you wake up, you have to find ways to receive motivation to get you going, get the engine running and the train moving.

Over the years I have tried many things, and some of them work and some get old really quick. One thing that will never work is getting extra sleep. Waking up early—way early—before work helps you start your day in a much less demanding environment. Waking up and feeling rushed or bombarded with tasks is not a good way to start your day.

I live literally three minutes away from the school where I work. I could almost throw a rock from my apartment to the school. Yet I wake up three hours before I have to go to work. This motivates me in many ways and is part of my self-care regimen. It helps me realize that my day does not begin and end at school. I have a home. I have a life. The great Dolly Parton said, "Don't get so busy living that you forget to make a life."

Sometimes I wake up and finish a movie or watch a movie. It makes me feel like I have a little control of my life. Now this is not for everyone, because I know a lot of people love sleep. I'm not one. If waking up early is not your thing, it may be music, dancing or exercise motivational videos, meditation, or reading. It does not matter as long as it puts you in a better mood and gets you ready for that day.

There will be things you might want to do in the morning, and as an adult it is at your discretion, but I would firmly advise you to not start your day with a joint (or any type of drugs, for that matter). It could cause you to lose your job and may really affect your mental clarity in the wrong way.

There have been recent studies showing that a lot of teachers have gotten themselves on antidepressants. My question is, what factors play a pivotal role in getting them to that point? What is at the root of that fruit? We have to address how we feel and gain control. No one wants to rely on anything for their happiness, although I know many of us are diagnosed with things that have grown out of our control. For those of us who have not yet allowed things to get out of control, let's try and maintain that control.

Music motivation is a great way to gain confidence in the job or task you are preparing to do. In order to feel like a superhero, you have to think like a superhero. Even sports players have headphones on as they walk into a sports arena. Music is one of the bigger motivations of this generation. Professional sports and even presidents use music to help them with their entrance, and it sets the stage for how they might feel about what they are doing.

Why can't teachers do this same thing? Get lit, as the kids say, whether you are playing "Eye of the Tiger" or Phil Collins's "In the Air Tonight." Play your music and play it loud. Let it move you and motivate you to the place you want to be: that headspace that makes you as powerful as a lion about to go hunting.

Let's practice like we play. If we want good to come *out* of us, first good must go *into* us. How we motivate ourselves is how we are going to be able to connect with kids and motivate them. Don't do or practice anything you can't share with the kids if one day they are feeling as down as you. Since you can't pass the joint to them, you might as well not smoke it. And this goes for anything else you are not allowed to share with the kids.

Questions for Self-Reflection

1. Who do you need to be to become more motivated?

2. What is the biggest challenge you face in the morning, and how can we make that easier for you?

3. What can we do to better prepare for each day to have the best approach possible (additions and takeaways)?

4. What's your willpower like? When is it strong, weak, or not noticed?

HEALTHY HABITS

In this world, I have come to the conclusion that there has to be a science to this life of mine. Meaning I cannot, as one author puts it, go on being dragged through life kicking and screaming, thinking there has to be another way. Well, there is—there is a science to living, and it's called healthy habits. If you have many, you will also have many good days. I look at it in this way: "What I do today is a direct investment to my tomorrow." What I eat, what I drink, whom I speak to, and what I speak to myself—all of these things affect my tomorrows.

I could sit here all day long and tell you the many things that I believe are healthy habits that could directly change the quality of your life, but if you do not discover this on your own, new information would do you no good. There has to be a great discovery made by you and you alone—no one else can see this through for you. George Bernard Shaw quotes:

> People are always blaming their circumstances for what they are. I don't believe in circumstances. The people who get on in this world are the people who get up and look for the circumstances they want, and, if they can't find them, make them.

Healthy habits are defined as any consistent behaviors that benefit your physical, mental, and/or emotional health. Healthy habits are just not as useful when they are only said, such as New Year's resolutions. Some people keep theirs for a week, some for a month, some for a few months, but I have yet to find someone who has kept it for a full year. Healthy habits come with discipline and accountability.

There are so many ways to define healthy habits, and to each their very own. But they are needed to make our life more complete and to help us accomplish our life goals. What I mean by this is when you have healthy habits, you have more days that you feel well than days that you don't. With that being said, healthy habits are the beginning of happiness.

Some of the educators I have worked with over the years have had horrible habits. I say horrible only because most led to some sort of stress, whether mental, physical, or emotional. The one habit I see much too often is the one most of you start your day with: the habit of drinking coffee. Look at this from a mental point of view. Every morning you wake up and you repeat the famous quote, "Don't bother me until I have had my coffee." What is this telling your brain, you might ask? That you cannot fully start your day until you have had a cup of coffee. This may not be true for a lot of you, and I may be making a false claim, but for those of you who are the type of person I am describing, you are only getting your mind addicted to something it really never needed.

Some of you may beg to differ because you make the assumption that drinking coffee is good for you, and under certain circumstances it can be. However, in America we are drinking a coffee that is old, stale, and dead, and has no real health benefits. So, for those of you who are a coffee-drinking machine, I suggest you stop cold turkey, and when you stop, make sure you are off work because it will come with withdrawals if you are an avid drinker: headaches, very low energy, and constant cravings. It's not an easy habit to kick to the curb, and the battle is mostly mental, not physical, because that's where it began for most of us.

I started drinking coffee when I was about twenty, and I remember my very first sip. It was awful, but I was hooked.

I was walking around the school asking teachers how they stay awake throughout the day—don't judge me! I was working two jobs at the time and going to school. This was how the mental addiction was starting to play out, and this would soon lead to a firm foundation of false belief.

Most of them said the same thing: Go to the teacher's lounge and grab a cup of coffee, and as I stated in self-care, advice from the wrong group of people is no help. I made my coffee and I added as much sugar and creamer as I could to dilute the coffee taste (that's the only way I will drink my coffee). It actually worked; I was wired as the day moved forward! I didn't too much enjoy the taste, but having energy was worth it.

Day in and day out I was drinking about three cups a day, but why not just one? Because I was crashing multiple times a day.

Drinking coffee may seem like a good habit because it's just a drink—and I'll say, *real* coffee (no sugar, no creamer, within the seven days of expiration after the beans have been roasted) is considered a super food. However, the coffee we drink is not only stale, but also dead, and it is manufactured for that purpose—a longer shelf life, a more sufficient product in this economy. So, for starters, the beginning of healthy habits starts with cutting away old, bad ones.

This is just one of the many habits I think, as an educator, you might need to consider changing. Look up the information for yourself and believe me when I say your body will have more energy without it. Your body does not ask for too much to function; out of all the vitamins in the world there are only thirteen essential vitamins that your body requires, most of which you can get from one cooked egg per day. The body also has never needed sugar, so don't think it's any benefit to you. You can live a full, better life without it.

Healthy habits do not start when you say it; it starts when you decide to cut out something but also fill the void. I can go around stopping this and stopping that, but if I am not starting anything to take its place then I won't stay with it.

Let's say I stop drinking coffee, but I add in more water. Or if I decided to watch less television, maybe I'll read more. Immediately, I'm replacing one for the other. Do it in small regiments, too, because if you reach too far, you might give up. Like one day I'm a meat eater and the next I try to be a full-blown vegan—that will never work, not even for your stomach. Adding in more vegetables a day is how it's done until your plate becomes full of them.

Healthy habits are not just eating better, because, as I said before, it is defined as mental, physical, and emotional health. So, let's talk about that mental health for a moment.

When teaching children, just getting a degree is not enough. Some of the best educators I have seen had no degree. What you put into your head is what's going to come out, and mental clarity comes from starting healthy habits.

When I was young, I used to imagine my teachers had no life—it was full of reading and writing just so they could be smart enough to teach me. For the most part, teachers are forced to move in the direction of getting as much higher education as possible, and I've learned, since being in education, that it does not require that to be effective in a child's life.

I have no degree and I'm extremely good at what I do; I have been told many times over that I have a gift. I'll tell you, it only comes from me having mental clarity each day I walk through those doors. I read every day because I need to know things—new things—in order for me to give the children something they might not have had or known before. This leads to me feeling confident when I'm leading a lesson in front of them. I'm told so many good things about why reading is important, but you also have to have time to sit and read. Some teachers are just not able to conjure up that type of time yet. So, if reading has not become your thing, that's understandable. There are other things, too.

One thing in particular that I highly suggest is that we all use our phone less. I use my phone the least amount of time as possible. This has been one of the best things I could have done for my mental clarity. To this day, I am still receiving so many good results from using it less. The benefits were stacking up so rapidly, I decided to delete my social media just to gain more time.

Healthy habits for me started as I got rid of things I thought were not so healthy. Some of you may be people who have to add; I'm one that needs to subtract. My healthy habits only begin when my unhealthy habits end. Mental health also falls along the same lines as emotional health, and it's a leading study in America right now.

I believe that most of the stress that we all are experiencing is stemming from the same root: unhealthy habits. We are sleep deprived, overweight, sick, and just all-around emotionally unstable. In order to take control of your future, you have to take control of your present healthy habits. You need to start today, not tomorrow.

Questions for Self-Reflection

1. What are five things you could stop doing today to make room for healthier habits?
   - ___
   - ___
   - ___
   - ___
   - ___

2. What are five things you could start doing to replace the unhealthy habits?
   - ___
   - ___
   - ___
   - ___
   - ___

3. Do you think you could find and list three other teachers that will hold you accountable?
   - ___
   - ___
   - ___

HEALTHY RELATIONSHIPS

Healthy relationships are the state in which two or more concepts, objects, or people are connected, or the state of being connected. In the day and life of a human being, we are connected to many people, and all of the relationships count toward our perspective on life. It is important that like-minded people surround us more than any other.

Most of the lasting relationships in our life start at work—it's where you meet the people who have the most in common with you. It is very easy to make connections in places where you have to be all day every day. However, even in our workplace, we have to be weary of the relationships we form, because all of them are not healthy.

So, the question then becomes, what might you consider a healthy relationship, and what is not? Well, that's an easier question to ask than answer. Basically, you have to cultivate a healthy community of people.

Take it from the perspective of one of the greatest thinkers of our time, Jordan Peterson. In his book *12 Rules for Life,* rule number three was "Make friends with people who want the best for you." During this chapter, close to the end, he states, and I quote:

> It is for this reason that every good example is a fateful challenge, and every hero, a judge. Michelangelo's

> great perfect marble David cries out to its observer: "You could be more than you are." When you dare aspire upward, you reveal the inadequacy of the present and the promise of the future. Then you disturb others, in the depths of their souls, where they understand that their cynicism and immobility are unjustifiable. You play Abel to their Cain. You remind them that they ceased caring not because of life's horrors, which are understandable, but because they do not want to lift the world up on to their shoulders, where it belongs.
>
> Don't think it is easier to surround yourself with good, healthy people than with bad, unhealthy people. It's not. A good, healthy person is an ideal. It requires strength and daring to stand up near such a person. Have some humility. Have some courage. Use your judgment, and protect yourself from too-uncritical compassion and pity.
>
> Make friends with people who want the best for you.

Too often in the school system I run into teachers that are sick and tired of being sick and tired. Others that are broken down, busted, and disgusted, and a few that just really hate their job. These are the people that, unfortunately, we are surrounded by all day and choose to be with outside of school at times. If we are not building each other up, what is the point of our fellowship?

While working as a store manager, I learned a lot about my employees, but the one thing I took with me as I walked out of the doors is that there are different types of workers: lazy, fun, loving, manipulative, drama kings and queens, bossy, outgoing, outspoken, hard-working, liars, authentic, rule-breakers, slackers, and overachievers, overreactors, over-compensators, overexcited, and those who are just plain-out over it. The funny thing about this is they all complain in their own way.

With this being said, you may now be able to see there is a

clear atmosphere for many different emotions to come about. That is why it is necessary for a clear line drawn in the sand for manifesting lasting productive relationships that complement who you are trying to become. You need healthy relationships whether you want them or not. A job might provide a space for many people to gather for the same cause, but you have to dictate if the relationship is beneficial.

When people have good relationships at work, the place is fun and exciting to be at. You look forward to going and are sometimes sad to leave. We all love it when we are surrounded by people that get us, because how often is it that anyone really listens to what you have to say? If you surround yourself with people who are like you, you get to experience connectivity every day.

Now, the trouble with this is that sometimes just because people share your space doesn't mean you share the same vision. Some people truly come into your life just for the company—that's all. You can never assume people are good just because they can relate. I'm sure there were a lot of people who could relate to Hitler when he wrote his book and talked of how Germany was stolen from its people. But I guarantee you that some of those same people would have never expected him to go as far as he did.

Like-minded people can be dangerous, but sometimes you can also be motivated by these people.

For me, I am a morning person—an ultra-morning person—and I enjoy being awake and walking into my place of work, but there are a lot of teachers that dread getting up in the morning and would rather me not be in their faces so early, so I've been told. So, I chose to find other people that were like me and were morning people because, for a person like me, I need that need met. I want to know that someone is just as happy about being up as I am and there is no place they would rather be. This is better for me than to be with those that do not. Why? Because they just don't get it.

Healthy relationships also level you out. My uncle once told me after he came out of prison that I leveled him. That meant the world to me to hear—that I was a person who helped him see the world in his preferred view.

It is so easy to get away from our purpose when others that do not share the same passion surround us. I've had times when I was around teachers that were complaining about students all the time, and in order to feel somewhat acceptable, I complained, too. It's not my thing at all—I'd rather work a twelve-hour shift than complain about why I was called in on my day off. You need healthy relationships that will level you out so you can, at all times, be challenged to become the person you are trying to be. Your time is extremely important, and you can no longer waste it with people that have a negative perspective when compared to yours.

Lifestyles will also affect who we become and choose to be around. There is a quote I like to use: "We don't buy the same wine!" There have always been teachers around me that made three times the amount I did (sometimes more than that). So, due to the fact that we made such vastly different amounts, our problems were different.

For example, if they were having a conversation about buying four new tires, soon I might be having a conversation about buying one used tire. Now, is this good or bad? It's up to you. I am the type of person where a social group and their ideas or way of life does not affect mine. Some of you might find yourself at times having FOMO, which actually stands for "fear of missing out," so these are the types of situations you need to see yourself out of. Hanging out with people who make more than you will always affect you in some way, and most of the time it is your bank account that is affected. But that is a later topic that we will discuss more of.

You are going to be connected with people always, but you have to manage the benefits of the relationships in order for you to consider if it is healthy or not.

Now this might be on your mind: would an intimate relationship be considered healthy at my place of work? I'll just say, it has never worked for me and most people that I know. Though intimate relationships are amazing and they have their place in our day, they may not be the best for a workplace. You want relationships that you can take a break from because you are constantly trying to figure out who you are and how you want to live, so I am not going to make suggestions, but I am going to say I prefer not to.

Whomever you work for does not care about you finding a healthy relationship—that is for you and your personal life. It is your job to do your job, not to go to work looking for the right people to talk to, and if you just so happen to find some, good for you, great. Your personal life is where you will have the most time to really build those lasting relationships that don't have a time limit. Start a social circle instead of social media; this will allow you to meet different people. Church is a great way to form lasting, healthy relationships and the one I would suggest the most.

In *The Purpose Driven Life,* written by Rick Warren, he speaks of this by saying:

> Only the Holy Spirit can create lasting relationships between believers, but he cultivates it with choices and commitments we make. Paul points out this dual responsibility when he says, "You are joined together with peace through the spirit, so make every effort to continue together in this way." It takes both God's power and our effort to produce a loving Christian community.

Church is full of honesty and real life all at the same time. And when you have a lot of healthy relationships, you have a healthy life.

When I first began my job at the Georgia Network of Therapeutic Education (GNETS) I was trained and worked with the most wonderful woman. We were both believers, and the classroom was run under the authority of God the Father, which meant what was best for the kingdom was best for the classroom. To this day we are the best of friends and constantly bring up our experience in the classroom. Day in and day out, we were faced with many challenges that we overcame through prayer and action. There is not a day that goes by that I do not use some the tactic that we explored in that classroom as it relates to the early-childhood development of students facing adversity in the home.

In this day and age, we struggle with making friends and we expect too much from those we decided would be our friends. We need to relearn how to make friends. I've heard so many people say, "I don't have any friends," as if it is a cool thing to say, but that only means you are lonely. People can be the perfect mirror to show you all of the things that you are lacking or just what you might need to grow in. Quality people will always bring the best out of you.

I do not know where my mental health would be if I didn't have a tribe of my own. We go out, have game nights, spend holidays together, talk to one another on the phone or in a coffee shop. We do life together. We don't put a strain on each other's time. We are not demanding, either; we see each other when we see each other, and that is what makes friendships so healthy. My friends and I are very open-minded toward one another; we are conservative in our own nature, but liberal for the sake of the group. We all are different, which makes it wonderful to hear stories from one another.

What we can become fully depends on who we are around. Make every relationship count. You need this from you!

Questions for Self-Reflection

1. Name five people currently in your social group.
   - ______________________________
   - ______________________________
   - ______________________________
   - ______________________________
   - ______________________________

2. Name one way each of these people directly benefits who you would like to become.
   - ______________________________
   - ______________________________
   - ______________________________
   - ______________________________
   - ______________________________

3. Is there anyone who does not need to be in your social group? If so, write a brief description of why.

____

____

____

____

____

SOCIAL LIFE

Social life is defined as the part of a person's time that is spent doing enjoyable things with others. There is something that needs to be made very clear for all the teachers around the world: YOUR JOB IS NOT YOUR SOCIAL LIFE! Where you work is just your job. You are not allowed, as human beings, to build your life around a job; that creates a lot of regret. You start to regret how your time is spent. You regret the community you stay in. You sometimes even regret having kids because you are sick of kids at times. Your job, though it may be the place you spend most of your days, should not interfere with your life. When you clock out for the day, that part of your life needs to be over.

As teachers, so much of your day is spent in the school building. All of your time goes into paper work, conferences, and paper work, grades, and more paper work. The funny thing is, when you signed up for this job there were only two things on the minds of most of you: This may be the easiest way out, or this should be a really safe career. Let's face it, we hope that the United States of America will always need teachers, but that may not always be the case.

So, how do you manage your time so that you are able to have more time for a social life, discipline, and desire? You have to want to have a social life and you have to make time for it. Thinking it is okay for you to sit at a school all day and only chat with the people you work with in and out of work is absurd. There is always more to life.

For me—and this is no lie—I might do one thing outside of school with other teachers one time every five years, but I make it very clear that when it is time for me to leave, I am gone. That means if you walk into my classroom after the day has ended, you only have a certain amount of time to talk and then I need you to close the conversation down. That is not even for my sake; that is for you. I want you to have closure so that when I walk out of that door you don't feel like I'm being rude. It may be an interesting conversation, but at that point, if it is about school, it does not interest me. When I leave the school I only have a few more hours to make the best out of my day, and I cannot let you have any part of that life.

The thing I have found to be most helpful is to arrive on time and leave on time. Do not live by "I'm the first one in and the last one out" cliché. The people that often say that are actually the first ones to burn out. When I arrive to the classroom at the beginning of the day, I take a look at all I need to get done, and right then and there I calculate exactly how much time it may take me to get all of it done. I set a time in my head, and I ask myself what might keep me from leaving at that time, and there is not one reason why I shouldn't. Discipline comes when you are looking forward to something, or you are setting a goal for something you really want, and what person does not want to leave work?

So, how does a social life work after you have left your job?

Well, remember what we talked about in the last part: You have to have some healthy relationships already going; there is no social life without them. Find some friends, and plan to do things with your friends. This will always give you something to look forward to, and that will definitely help your mental clarity.

I hear so many people say way too often, "I do not have time for friends," and here I am trying to make more time for my friends. When I am making time for my friends, I'm looking for a neutral setting, something we both really don't mind.

I have a friend, and when he gets off work, his social life begins at the gym. He enjoys going and working out, but also walking around and talking to others. He used to always ask me to go to the gym with him, but that is not my thing; I hate the gym. So, don't just join someone for the heck of it—you need a social life and not a social strain. It's always good to be in good company, and my friend is a very nice person that I do enjoy spending time with, but we do not find life in the same things.

Social media is not a social life. When you get on the computer, phone, tablet, anything that requires Wi-Fi, this is not a part of you being social and having a life. According to the research found on the Healthy.com, one of the ten problems with social media was this: Peer pressure is alive and well on social media, with adults as well as with teens, and what's interesting is that you may not even realize it's happening.

Making decisions based on what you might have been led into does not give you the power to find joy in that thing. Social media has become like the devil, literally, or just plain old sin in and of itself. My old youth minister used to say, "Sin will take you farther than you intended to go, keep you longer than you wanted to stay, and cost you more than you were willing to give." The drama can be addictive—don't get me wrong—but the joy of life can be equally as addictive, believe me. I deleted my social media for years, I began to paint, I started a nonprofit, and I wrote this book. You'll be amazed of the life you can have after social media. And for those of you who have gotten so addicted that you are on it at work, shame on you.

I don't care how many messages you respond to or likes you get on your pictures, this is not a healthy social life. And why, you might ask? Because anything you can do at your job cannot bring you full pleasure. When you are at your job, you need to be working, not on any social-media platforms, because, though it may seem like it makes the day go by faster, it does not. It slows down your productivity and leads to stress as it relates to finishing other work. You need that productivity; that's your key out of the door. Don't take coffee breaks and bathroom breaks. Work until the day ends, and watch how much time you leave with.

Social media is not only a waste of your time, but going back to those feelings of missing out, they start in a place where you don't wholeheartedly want to be. Now, we all like our jobs, but I don't care where you work, vacation always looks better. All we see on social media are things we would love to be doing and we could be doing if it were not for us always watching other people doing it.

You have to desire to do more with your life. Start today—your social life will begin when you take an action step toward it. Make a conscious effort to plan ahead so you can think about these things throughout your day and they can excite you.

Most of all, go, see, and do, as my mentor always tells me. You have to get out of the house to have a social life. You can save all the money you want for whatever you want, but things don't come with happiness; they are empty and lifeless. If you want to have a life, spend your money on life. Save for outings with friends and not new shoes or a shirt. Save for a vacation that lasts a long time instead of redoing your porch.

Remember, to get to the place where you are having a pretty good social life, you need the discipline and the desire, and it does not take much to get them. The only person that is stopping you from having a social life is you—not your family, not your job, just you.

Just wait until you begin to add more fun into your life, what it will do to your laugh, and smile, and overall health. When you begin to feel the difference in your moods, you will wonder how you ever lived without it.

Remember when you were a kid and you could just sit, and watch a movie, and enjoy it because that's all you were thinking about? Or as a kid, when you ate food, you enjoyed it, mostly because you were not thinking about how much it was going to cost you? Your social life will help you get back to that place where you have less worry and you feel like a kid again.

There is a quote in a special edition of *Time* magazine about mental health, and the quote was the very first thing you read when you open the pages: "YOU SPEND YOUR LIFE AN INCH AWAY FROM MADNESS," in all caps, just like that. I do not discredit their findings, either, but I will say this, in all caps, "YOU SPEND YOUR LIFE AN INCH AWAY FROM THE KINGDOM OF HEAVEN ALSO!" Jesus said it was as close to you as your hand. Give up all that you have so that you can receive all that you need.

Questions for Self-Reflection

1. How are you going to make time to leave the school earlier than usual?

2. What is holding you back from having a really great social life?

3. How many of your friends are from work?

4. When will you delete your social media completely?

5. How will you begin to spend your money on life instead of lifeless things?

____

____

____

____

____

Financial Independence

Financial independence is the status of having enough income to pay one's living expenses for the rest of one's life without having to be employed or dependent.

Money—one of the heaviest chains attached to our souls, the one thing that has enough control over us mentally, physically, and emotionally. Money dictates how hard we will work and how long. Money tells us what to wear and eat, and how to spend our time. Money makes us sad, angry, and confused, and the biggest lie it tells us is that it will bring us freedom. I heard a quote once that said, "Money makes the unimportant things easy and the important things hard."

Well, all this is true, and in order to get to a place of financial freedom, you have to free yourself from finances. Control the desired outcome and you'll control the income.

We all know teaching is one of the hardest jobs in the world, and yet it is also one of the lowest paid jobs when considering the work that is being done. There are more jobs in this world that pay way more than teachers. Even I was bound to make more flipping pizza . . . way more. So, if your decision to get into teaching was motivated from the thought of making easy money, you better rethink.

So, my guess is now you are asking, "Then how will we ever gain financial freedom, and is it even possible?" I'm not here to sell you on something I know that you cannot do; I'm here to tell you what I know you can. You're right—with student debt, kids, mortgage, car, food, water, shelter, you have nothing left to give at the end of the month when it comes to your paycheck. God forbid you get a flat tire or need to call a plumber. Extra money just does not exist in the life of a teacher, but we are not bound to that level of thinking. It is a fact that you might make only a certain amount of money, but there are endless possibilities in what you decide to do with it.

I'm reminded of a quote said in the greatest book ever written in my personal opinion: "The kingdom of heaven is like a treasure hidden in a field. When a man found it, he hid it again, and then in his joy went and sold all he had and bought that field" (Matthew 13:44, NIV). At this current moment in my life, I do not make much at all, but I've been able to make it work. There are things I have to do mentally to prepare myself for financial freedom, and one of the first things is to always remember what I make is what I make, and right now I can do nothing about that. There is nothing in this world I need other than food, water, shelter. The rest is extra. I do not allow my emotional world to dictate how I materialize my physical world.

Let me break that down for you.

Imagine something you wanted that you now have. Go back to how you felt when you bought it and how you feel about it now, and then ask yourself, "Did I really need it?" I don't care who you are, the answer will always be *no*. Our emotions are the cause and effect of what we buy. How you feel can no longer control how you spend. The key is to leave your emotions in the car. This stuff is not alive and it can do nothing for the living. When you find that treasure that the great book talks about, you are finding a new understanding. Your treasure is a new way of life.

When I quit my job as a store manager at a local pizza restaurant, I had to rethink my life because I no longer had the income to go to different restaurants every day, spend $300 shopping—even filling up my car had become a challenge. I was broke and financially in chains because my emotions were telling me I could no longer live happily.

I would walk into a store and I could tell you a million things that I just knew I needed, and I could imagine how my life was going to change when I got them. That part is where my emotions were getting involved, and the question was no longer if I needed it or not, it was, "Do I have enough to buy it?" I'm not talking about did I have enough to buy the things and have money left to eat—no, *did I have enough to just buy the thing*? If I had $15 left for two weeks, I'd spend the whole $15 on what it was that I wanted. I was the definition of an impulsive buyer, and there were millions of others just like me!

So, how did I break this habit? I had to find more fulfilling ways to spend what little I had, and it was not hard to do as long as I was thinking about those fulfilling things. Out of sight, out of mind—in sight, in mind!

In order to change this habit of impulsive buying, you have to form new habits, and these new habits have to become natural. There are a few things I do that have become the norm and have completely changed my bank account.

First things first, pay your debt. When a person has debt, that is a physical burden that they can see. They see the interest go up, and that puts a strain not only on your account, but also on your emotions. Because money burns the pocket, burn in on your bills first.

When I get my check, I buy nothing until I pay all my bills first, and after that, I don't even want to spend anything else because it all went out so quick in the first place. After that, I try to strategically plan out how the rest of my money will be spent. If I know what I have specifically, I know what the budget is. It's like a grocery list—if you go without one, you'll always spend more because you'll get what you don't need.

Now, saving will be the hard part because who wants to save? But I have found out that it is important. However we try to blindly save, always save for something. Your emotions need to see something physically to save for so it is able to reach toward that and have deadlines. You might save, but if you are saving for nothing then you are just waiting to spend it on something.

The debit card was the best and the worst thing for human beings because we cannot see what we spend and how it adds up when we spend. Get cash and leave the card. As it becomes a lifestyle, you will immediately feel the effects and your material world will look a lot different. You don't have to keep up with anyone; what you have is what you have, and there will always be someone in the world who is living off much less than you. So, if there is anyone else who can live with less, then so can you.

You also need to keep in mind that there is a current system in place and studies are done on how to create impulse buyers. They don't care if you make $5 per day—their goal is to separate the consumer from every dollar they make. For example, when you are in line at retail stores, there is that section right before you get to the register. That section, believe it or not, is called "impulse buys," and they are everywhere. These are the things we buy just for the heck of it, and we do it right before we have almost made it out of the door.

When you walk out of your house, they know exactly what you like. It is almost as if they know you better than yourself—what colors, what sales, what you like to eat. They know if they can make it convenient enough, they can get you to buy it, sadly even if it is trash. You need to be three steps ahead of them at all times in order to keep your financial freedom.

Whatever that man found in that field, it was worth giving up his current mindset, and he knew it would lead him to so much more. Money plays such a huge part in our life, but we need to take off the blinders so that we are able to see the stigma connected to it. If you allow yourself to take off these chains alone, you see that there is a whole world around you, and it is breathtaking.

Just imagine how it is going to feel when you can go in a store and walk around for hours just to buy nothing, leaving the house with $100 and coming back home with the same. On top of that, going out and doing stuff instead of just going shopping—it's almost as if that is all we know how to do these days. Go sit at a lake, take a walk, go swimming. There is much more to life than just making money and spending it; there is everything in between. And you deserve it!

Questions for Self-Reflection

1. How much of your check is truly yours after you get it?

2. What would you do if you found you had extra money?

3. How much could you save if you saved for one year?

4. When will you really begin to pay off all your debt?

5. Let's start strategically planning how we will spend every penny! As an exercise, take a blank sheet of paper, write down the total amount you will make at the end of this month, and create ways to spend every penny, even if that spending is saving!

In Conclusion

This concludes Part 1, consisting of what you need from you to be successful around the kids. Now, keep in mind, that part was largely about you, but make no mistake, it's all for the kids. You are the most important piece to their complex mental puzzles, but you have to be taken care of first.

Consider this short story written by me, if you would.

The Boy, the Farmer, and the Horse

Almost like the horse and the racer.

Once there was a boy, seventeen years of age, who lived in a small town with a very poor family. His dad did not make much at all, and they could hardly afford to eat every night. Their life was hard.

His parents decided that it was time for the boy to do his part around the house, so his dad introduced him to this farmer that he knew who needed the extra help, and the boy began work the next morning. The father took his son and introduced him to the farmer, and before the father left the boy, he told him, "Every penny you make goes straight to me."

The boy understood and began his work.

It was the perfect idea: the boy was making enough to get lots of extra food for the house. His father could not have been prouder of his son and the way things were going for their family.

Things were going so well that his parents decided to have another baby. At this point, life could not have been better. The boy and the farmer had a good relationship, too; the boy was a very hard worker, and the farmer knew.

One day, the boy decided to ask the farmer how he made his money, and he told him, "Horse racing." The boy was intrigued; he wanted to know more and more about it. Every day he'd ask more questions, and the farmer would tell him more stories.

The boy asked if he could teach him how to train horses, to which the farmer was happy. He decided to let him train one of the newer horses born recently. This was the smallest horse in the stable at the time. He taught the boy everything he knew, and the boy was in love with the horse because the horse had so much potential. The horse began to do races and would win very often; the farmer was very pleased with the results.

Three years later, while the boy was working with the farmer, a man came to give the farmer a huge offer for the horse. The farmer told the boy and also added he would be willing to split the profits since he trained the horse and all. But the boy was not ready to part ways, and to postpone the deal, he offered to race the horse himself if the farmer would keep him. So, the farmer decided to keep the horse and allow the boy to be the racer.

More and more wins came about, and a deeper bond between the boy and the horse ensued. The farmer was making money, the boy was making money, and the horse belonged to the farm, so the farm was making money.

Another offer was made for the horse, and at this point the boy and the horse had made a name for themselves. But this was the biggest offer the farmer had ever received.

The boy was a man now, and the journey with this noble steed was over. The farmer sold the horse and the young man was broken. The farmer went and sat down with the boy and talked. He told him that over the years he tried to teach him everything he knew about horse training, but the lesson about parting ways with these animals was something he had to learn from experience.

He told the boy that was the longest time he had ever kept a horse besides his own first training horse. He said, "You can put your soul into these horses, but you cannot get attached. What you did was exactly how you are supposed to train a horse—love it, take care of it, make it feel as if the animal is your whole world. And because of that, it took care of you. It exceeded anything any horse has ever done here in my stables. You made a real champion.

"The horse may never perform for anyone else like he did for you, and that's the problem. You have to understand, young man, this is a business and these horses belong to the business. We have to let nature take its course for them as well as us. Though it might have felt like yours and you might have treated it like yours, it never belonged to you. This is a business, and you will have to learn how to train every horse like that and be able to part ways sooner or later."

In this story, you might be thinking which part you play in this narrative. Well, the racer/trainer. This is your character because you are teaching the horse/the student everything they know. The boy was always the most important part of the horse's life; not even the mother of the horse could have prepared the horse for what was going to come of his life. In order for the boy to make that horse perform like it did, he had to be with it every step of the way, making sure it learned what it needed to. In the process, he also had to love the horse as if the horse was his own, and he developed a passion for training horses by doing so.

The farmer taught the young man everything he knew, but not all things. The business side of things that the young man had no clue about he had to learn on his own. The point I need you to take from this is, you and the student are one and without students there are no schools to teach at. It may seem like a lot to take in, but at the end of the day, it's set up like a business.

Your family and friends may have told you, "Do not get into teaching. There is no money in it." And they were absolutely right, but you still made that decision and here you have to live with it.

The farm was the school you work in, and your principal is the farmer. His only job is to make sure you perform at the highest level you can and give you the experiences you need to do so. Your principal cannot teach you all there is to know about teaching children and developing a professional partnership in order for the students to continue to thrive without you in their life.

He also can't teach you how to part ways with your students after putting so much into them and getting so much out of them, because this is something you have to learn on your own. You have to love them like they're your own, but be ready to let go of them when the time comes. This is one of the hardest lessons to learn, but once it is learned, you can do what you need to do to help these children.

The horse was only as good as his trainer. In order to see the classroom as you should, perform as you should, and be successful, you have to take care of you first. Your emotions, finances, free time, eating habits, energy levels, and more—you need to do all the things you read in Part 1, because this is important for you and the students, but mostly the students.

How can you walk into a school and give what you don't have? How can you teach if you are not mentally present? From here on out, in order to make a difference, you have to be different!

Part 2

What the School Needs from You . . .

This part of the book will be very different than the first, and much shorter. In this part, what I would like for you to keep in mind is, you are part of a system or machine. This system or machine does not work unless you have all that you need to allow the machine to use you in the way that you are needed. It is extremely important for you to accept the fact that you are not in control of your path completely when it comes to working for the system. You might think you are because you have your own classroom, but there are still rules that must be followed in order for things to go smoothly.

Furthermore, we live in an ever-changing world inside of an existential vacuum. The outer world is continually affecting our inner world, and just when you believe you have a grip on things, it changes again.

So, in order to get ahead of the curve, you literally have to just join the curve. There are concepts that you may not like, but no matter your personal opinion of things to come, it is only when you accept that you are not in control that you truly become in control.

This sounds crazy, but working within the parameters that someone has already set before you is always the easiest way to get ahead. Over the years, I have had the privilege of working with some of the best teachers in the game, and they all shared a commonality: it never failed. They followed the rules to a T and moved forward based on what they knew needed to be done; they rarely complained about it and always did their best. This is what the school needs from each and every one of you: Try not to complain, and always do your best.

Within the rules, there can always be success. The trouble is, sometimes people just don't follow the rules. Not following the rules creates conflict within and out.

For example—and I'm only using this because this is the only readily available truth that I personally have to offer and have experienced—most people find it very hard to find any joy in being a so-called Christian because they believe that it calls them to be perfect. Well, that is so far from the truth. Why bother to bring it up? The Bible gives us instructions about how God intended for us to live out this life in peace and prosperity with one another. Many believe that the rules and regulations of the Bible were meant to make God happy and us miserable, but that is not the case.

I believe that God made such rules so that we might live among one another with joy and thanksgiving. To think that the rules were for him makes no sense—they were for us because he already knew how we could get toward one another while being a lone ranger.

The same goes for the school system: the rules were set so that you might get the most out of your experiences with the children. Once you follow the rules as they were written, you can begin to enjoy your job, much like the rules of the Bible. If followed—truly followed—you can begin to live out your life on this earth with joy.

To Be Present

To be present is defined as being in a particular place, and what would a school be without their teachers? If someone were to walk up to you with a job offer and say something like, "Hey, I need you to babysit thirty-eight to forty kids for me starting at seven a.m. to three p.m., and I'll pay you at the end of the month. By the way, Monday through Friday," that would sound crazy and probably end with a resounding *no* from anyone. Teachers are being referred to as the new glorified babysitters. That, my friend, is a glorified lie.

So, how are they able to be present day in and day out, and do their job with all that being said? Because, again, you are heroes.

Being present at your job does not just mean something to your boss, but the children you work with, too. From their perspective, to know someone is interested in seeing them every day is something that is not so common in our society today; kids have a better relationship with you than with their own parents.

When you show up to work every day, just allow yourself to remember not all the children may be excited to see you, but I guarantee there is one child that is looking forward to you being there. It has been said many times that the only thing that keeps some children in school is the fact that they have a good, productive relationship with someone in the school. You being present is very important to their future and livelihood.

I can remember working for a school where teachers were calling out of work left and right, there were turnovers, and the school was chaos. Classrooms were so dysfunctional, you would not believe what would go on. The lead teachers always had something to do, and they did not mind calling out to do so. Relatively speaking, we were a small school of about ten classrooms, and some days over half of the lead teachers were out. I'm afraid to say it never got better, even after I resigned from my position.

So, why is it that not being present is so ineffective? Well, there are three reasons why not being present can affect the growth of a particularly well planned–out class: The teacher is the only one that will ever be able to truly enforce the rules because they were the ones who made the rules. Rules are meant to be followed, and based on the teacher, the rules have been catered to his or her style of teaching.

The second reason we have to consider is that the teacher is the only one who fully knows the personality of each and every one of their students. Another teacher or a substitute will not understand what it takes to engage a particular student. So, knowing the students is major when it comes to addressing behaviors, and the only way to know your students is to be present.

The third and final thing is that if you are not present, chances are you will get behind on all of the major paper work and grades that need to be turned in. Getting behind is a major setback in a classroom, and some teachers never get the opportunity to catch back up.

So, as a teacher, if you are not able to be anything else for your students, please at least be present. If not for them, be present for you, because you made the commitment to be there on time and ready to work when you signed the contract. Work as if you are being watched 100 percent of the time—just maybe you are.

When we really take a deeper look at being present, what we are really talking about is just being **available**—not occupied, free to do something. Showing up to work on time is only half the battle; showing up period is the other half.

The school's success is based on how often you show up to work. Showing up is a part of ratio, professionalism, and the overall foundation of the school. To me, there are a million things you can add to a school day to improve the learning environment of your students, but at the end of the day, nothing is more important than you, the teachers. If they are there, they make up a huge percentage of the population in the school. So when teachers are unavailable, things can become pretty hectic.

Ratio is how many students to educators you have in a classroom setting. Ratios can change depending on a higher or lower student population. When teachers are there and prepared to work, ratios can remain intact, but when so many teachers call out in one day, that becomes a problem.

The national average public-school student to teacher ratio is approximately 16:1, the lowest being 11:1 and the highest being 23:1. If you have 2,500 students in a school, you will need at least 108 teachers at all times to keep the numbers within ratio. Now, of course, there are going to be students and teachers out on a daily basis, but this number needs to remain in place for the majority of the school year.

If you are one of those teachers who is constantly throwing off the ratio, then it is your fault that more teachers need to be hired. The schools need you to be available because that's what makes a school a professional environment. It is a part of your professionalism to be there when you have signed a contract to be there.

A machine can only be as good as its working parts. As a teacher, you are a part of a huge machine. Not only does this machine mold the future, but it controls the success of it. If you want your students to be professionals, you have to set the standard.

No building can go under construction without first having a foundation laid out, and the building will only be as strong as the foundation. If certain pieces used for the foundation are not available on the construction site, how else can building start?

For every day that things are missing, that's another day behind and we have lost progress at that point.

Being available also means that you're not only physically available, but also emotionally. This means that you are there for any emotional needs that the child may have aside from your own. Not to throw any shade at the school counselor we have all been referred to, but if we are going to be honest, none of us has ever come back with sound advice. We have an emotional obligation to these students because we are with them the majority of the day. How could we not be there for them?

I can remember working with a student that was very troubled. His emotional needs were not being met, so that affected his work ethic. He would come to school, and he did not want to work, and he caused most of the disruptions throughout the day. I wasn't sure what his needs might have been at the time, but because of the emotions he was showing, I knew I had to be patient. It was like I was walking down a hallway blindfolded: I didn't know anything, therefore I could not speculate. I just needed to be there when he was ready to talk about it.

Now this did not mean I cut him so much slack that we both lose; it just meant that I am not going to be as pressing as I normally am. I was present and patient for whatever emotional needs aside from my own personal agenda.

Being present also means you are not there looking at emails or browsing on your phone and the internet. How many times have you been teaching a lesson that you worked really hard on and it just seemed like none of the children were paying attention? How did that make you feel? That's what happens when a class is given busywork and the teacher decides this is a good time for them to take a break.

This is a pivotal period where the student needs you as a teacher to be present the most, because some of the children are not comfortable asking questions during the lesson. Some teachers have even gotten used to doing certain things like this and it has become a habit, almost to the point of planning it into their day. I've just so happened to walk by a classroom where the lead teacher and the aid are both looking at devices and the students are working. This is not being truly present.

Doing what needs to be done when it needs to be done can help in a big way. Answering emails is not something your job is hoping you get done before the end of the day. If you go into your class and there are no kids in the room, this is a good time to do extra work, but as soon as the children arrive, it is game time. Everything else needs to be put to the side to be done when they are not around. This way, you can be 100 percent present with them during the day.

Most bullying happens because a teacher was not paying attention. Being fully present can put a stop to bullying. If you are not able to find a particular time to get things done, then it may be good to preorganize your day.

Now, we all know people get sick, but there are some of you that need subs way too often. This is not being present, either. Some subs come into the school so much the students mistake them for certified teachers all the time. However, there is a difference. Subs are not good help for the students at all, and most of the time they don't even understand the work they are handing out.

So, without you being present, how are the students going to be able to learn anything that day? The students are losing a full school day of learning, and if you are out too many days, you may even have to reteach the entire lesson. It has been said that in forty-eight hours, 80 percent of the information we learn is lost if not revisited. Just let that sink in.

Kids also do not have any respect for a person they barely know. Subs get mistreated all of the time, and it's also not fair to them. They are placed in random classrooms and they are just trying to survive the day. Plus, who knows your students better than you? How can you not feel obligated to be there for them as much as possible?

You know exactly how to respond to each and every one of

your students, and that is only because you are there with them, getting to know them better and better as the year goes by. Your job needs you there for that particular reason. Just getting a body to cover you helps no one, not even you! The school cannot make you go to work; they can only ask and hope for you to show up, and when you do, things get done the way they should.

Being in your classroom is also important. Teachers should not be in the hallway conversing with their closest neighbor; it gives the children too much room to exploit the instructional time. Now, I'm sure this is not the result of every teacher in America, so if this is not you, don't take it personally. However, if it is, when you know better, do better.

So, back to these "glorified babysitters" you have been called so many times—I think we have arrived at an understatement. You go into that school every day just to be disrespected by someone else's child. And the kind of disrespect you receive, you don't even tolerate from your own kids.

When you are present for your day, you are aware of what the day is going to look like, and that is what makes you special. You know that the kids are not going to be great, the lunch is not going to be great, and the day may even drag by, but you are needed.

Society may act as if teachers are not needed by paying low wages and requiring more education, but we know you are needed. They may even add more paper work as if they are trying to run you off, but you are needed. There are no incentives in place for good teachers—you are just placed in a category of your own, your hard work is hardly noticed—but if you continue to be present in spite of it all, as a result a kid's life will be changed forever every single time you decide you are going to work!

Questions for Self-Reflection

1. How would you describe your punctuality and attendance when it comes to the school year?

____

____

____

____

____

2. How well would you say you know your students on a scale from one to ten (ten being very well and one being not well at all)?

____

____

____

____

____

3. What can you do to get to know your students better?

____

____

____

____

____

4. How has Maslow's hierarchy of needs affected your classroom?

____

____

____

____

____

5. Have you made yourself fully available and present for the school system?

____

____

____

____

____

To Be Trained and Experienced

Teachers are expected **to be trained** to teach a particular skill or type of behaviors through practice and instruction over a period of time. There is not a job on earth that would not want their employees to be trained.

I am hopeful that they will train you well when you get there. In teaching, it is pivotal—your school needs you to be trained. Maybe it's not the type of job where you could lose a finger, or a hand even, but you could lose your patience followed by your mind. So, when working with children, it is best that you get as much training as you can take. That alone is a personal feat because I believe teachers do not receive all the proper training they need before being thrown into a classroom.

Most teachers when starting at their school have never really worked a whole lot with children—well, as far as the ones I know. You go to college, do your certain number of student-teaching hours, and that is all. Fresh off the boat, they throw you to the sharks, and nowadays most teachers are not lasting more than five years. The more you are trained, the more you are able to manage your expectations, and the more kids you've been around, the more you can begin to manage their expectations also.

Studies say that children are precise indicators of what our society looks like in real time. Meaning they are so impressionable, you can tell what's going on in our world just by teaching in a classroom.

When I first started working in a classroom setting, what surprised me the most was how much the students did not know and how much I was expected to help them learn in one year. That is an ongoing conflict in our public schools today. While the parents are expecting the teachers to do absolutely everything, the children are doing absolutely nothing. I felt unprepared because there was so much that was needed and so little time to do it, and I was one of the ones responsible for what goes out into our society.

So many new teachers are walking into those same scenarios, and those meetings you desperately hate going to are the ones you need more often because some teachers ask questions that you never have thought of asking. That alone makes you better in the classroom; some schools even require them once or twice a month. In some meetings, the information is irrelevant to you and your students, but they still require you to go because it looks good. I've been in meetings where instead of building you up, they are tearing you down. Those are the meetings I despise the most—no training being done at all.

The truth of the matter is, schools can hardly come up with anything to prepare you for the kids you are encountering on a daily basis. Only time and training will tell—boots on the ground training, that is.

Teaching almost has to come naturally, and you have to desire to teach. A lot of teachers go wrong by assuming they have power just because they have power. You know the type: You walk in the classroom demanding the attention of the students while never taking the time to feel them out. You have an agenda to whip them into the shape they need to be in, but there is an order to it. You must first take your time and spend time with each and every individual student. Then once you know them, demand the attention.

The more time you are spending with kids, the better you are with kids. That is where most of an educator's training will come from. It counts as training when you stop a fight—maybe this time you took a few shots to the head, but the next time you may not. When you are getting cursed out by kids, this, too, is a part of your training, and how you react will either make you weaker to the students or stronger.

Every time a kid comes to school and looks as if they are not excited about their day and you try to give them words of encouragement, this, too, is a part of your training. When you actively step in and intervene on a situation without looking at it from a distance and saying, "They do not pay me enough for this," that is when you are being trained for free, and that is the best training you'll ever get.

Some teachers prefer to go out and get a master's degree as part of their training, and there is nothing wrong with that. Not only are they getting more educated on the most current research about the children they are influencing, but also getting a raise for doing so—sometimes a really significant one. Certifications also look good as part of your training. They are costly at times, but worth getting the extra experience.

There are many ways to become a better teacher for the kids, but most of what you are going to learn has to be done on your own time, effort, and money. You are pretty much going to have to volunteer yourself to the cause of raising other people's children.

However, there is a bright side to getting all of this training and experience, even if it costs you a fortune. In return you'll get to work the most rewarding and easiest job in the world. How could anyone refer to teaching as the easiest job in the world? Because it can be, if you are doing it right.

When you become good at something—and I'm not talking *kind of* good, I'm talking at least ten thousand hours good—you become a master, and everything else seems like free sailing. Some teachers have mastered the art of teaching and now they feel retired.

They won't tell you this, but there are teachers around you living like this. Jobs are only harder when you are not properly doing them. If you are starting out the wrong way, you will end up in the wrong place. When it comes to teaching, there is a Goldilocks place you get to from teaching at least ten to fifteen years—not too easy, not too hard, but just right. This is without any extra training, but with the proper training and experience, you could get to that stage in three to five years.

How awesome would that feel to really enjoy teaching and watching the students grow? This will only come if you are trained properly. That is why it is important to do your job right as often as you can; this will only make it get easier for you as the years go by.

Why spend the whole forty years of your teaching career miserable, looking forward to retirement? That is no way to live. Stop listening to all of those other negative teachers, the ones that just find a reason to complain every day. They are only complaining because they don't know what they are doing and they are too embarrassed to ask, so they complain. Be an advocate of your own personal growth and get all the training you need for your future and the future of our society.

Over time, your perception will change, and there will come a time when you will know that you are properly trained. That time will come when you realize that you are able to not only see the lesson from their point of view, but also the world. When you have spent enough time with children, you get a better understanding of their needs for success, and that is what it is all about. The training will always take you to that next level of thinking. You're going to be better at forecasting what is to come when things get a little out of hand in the class.

I remember we used to train for two weeks—and this was going to be your complete training for the entire year—and at the time I was working in an alternative school with kids dealing with trauma. The students were emotionally unpredictable: one moment they would be fine and then, before you know it, there are chairs flying around the classroom, literally. I'm not even sure if that school would have been able to come up with a training course that would have prepared me well enough to walk into a class and feel confident.

So, I'll say this: Some of the training you will receive will be of no use to you, only because you cannot predict how a student might behave on any given day.

Most of what we learned in those two weeks were how to get out of the way when a student becomes angry. We didn't really learn how to get them to learn anything; all we were doing was teaching each other "When this kid does this, you want to do that."

At another alternative school I worked at, we trained for four weeks before we even got to enter into a classroom, and this was a school that was also dealing with students and trauma. However, it was the same training—when the anger train has left the station, get out of the way. We were being tossed right into high-stress situations and had no warnings or even a safety protocol. After one year of getting beat up by the students, I decided this was no longer the place for me.

In all, when there seems to be no training offered and you truly love what you do and want to know more, read. For years I have been reading and researching everything there is to know about early-childhood development. This was for me, and as a result, it was for the job. Not only did my newfound knowledge give me a sense of job security, but also it helped my self-confidence in the classroom. For me, I just did not feel right leaving it up to the school to teach me everything I wanted to know; some of the stuff I just wanted to learn on my own.

If you have the time and the energy, I say go for it!

Questions for Self-Reflection

1. How many total hours have you had working with youth?

___

___

2. Do you think your school provides all the training you need, or could there be more?

___

___

___

___

___

3. Have you ever sought out training for your own personal growth?

___

___

___

___

___

4. How much training do you think is necessary for a brand-new teacher to be considered for a classroom (hours, weeks, months), and why?

___

___

___

___

___

5. Do you feel as if teaching comes to you naturally, or not yet?

To Be Punctual

Punctual is defined as happening or doing something at the agreed or proper time, on time.

If you have ever been late to anything, then you know how bad it can throw your day completely off. As soon as you walk into a job, or date, or anything late, there is almost no coming back mentally for you—at least that is what I have learned over the years about myself.

Being punctual is many things and it does not all have to do with just arriving on time, but turning in papers, setting up meetings, etc. So, when it comes to getting things done, your job needs you to be punctual. When you are all-around punctual, you are ready to begin the day as soon as your students walk in the door—no last-minute changes, nothing. This also adds a good productive workflow throughout the day.

When you are described in a meeting with other teachers, you do not want them to describe you as the teacher that is always physically late. So, what is it that makes us arrive late to work so very often?

How much of a gap are you leaving and are you within the margin of error? This is a very important question to consider when leaving home because there are many things that can affect your drive to work. Most people hardly ever take traffic lights, stop signs, and buses into account when on their way to work, and some do. But to be away from the margin of error, you should double the time you have to arrive at work, meaning if I need to be there by 7:30 and I live thirty minutes away, I need to leave at 6:30.

If you're an educator and you are having a hard time finding a reason to show up on time, think about the children. Schools are raising children to understand that being tardy is unacceptable, so why would you even dream of breaking that rule yourself? Being on time as an educator shows your students the importance of showing up on time, and any school that enforces this with consequences is doing the right thing in my book—literally.

When you are talked about in meetings, do you want your boss and coworkers to think of you as the one who never shows up on time? I think not. I'm sure none of the teachers reading this book have this problem, but I have to address it because I did.

I lived within walking distance of the school I worked in and I was always late. For me, I was well beyond the margin of error, but I took it for granted. I was never super late, but always late enough to feel like I needed a little more time to get a bit more prepared for the day. That is the feeling that I am actively trying to avoid these days, and that is the feeling that I believe we are falling into too often and not doing anything about it. We have to see it as a problem before it becomes a problem, and this is in regards to everything we do at the school.

Integrity is something that I decided not to cover, but I will briefly touch on the subject matter. Being honest is all we may have left in this world. Our word is our bond, as the phrase goes. I was late to my job most of the time because my boss hardly ever saw me go in. This made it easy to just say I was on time when I knew for a fact that I was not. Even though I was never caught in the action, what if I were? How embarrassing would that have been, and what would have been the consequences?

Your job needs you to show up on time because it is a part of your job description, and leaving work on time should be held to the same standards. Leaving work on time is also a part of you being punctual. They need you to work your full day with the least amount of excuses as possible. If you arrive early, that is your choice, but that may not be an excuse for you to leave early. Some jobs may require you to clock in. Therefore, if you do show up early, you may have the liberty of leaving early, but most teaching jobs are salaried, which means your school is not keeping up with your hours.

Lastly, if there were one thing I would advise you to avoid, it would be a no-call no-show. No job likes that, and schools shouldn't dare to allow it.

Be on time all the time.

Questions for Self-Reflection

1. Have you always arrived to work on time?

____
____
____
____
____

2. Has showing up to work on time ever been a problem for you?

____
____
____
____
____

3. Would you ever consider getting to work one or two hours early?

____
____
____
____
____

4. How has being punctual changed your life?

____
____
____
____
____

5. Are you known for being early, on time, or late?

To Be Drug-Free

Growing up we learned so much about living a drug-free life in school. I can remember that famous quote, "Just say no!" We were told that it could ruin our health and we could go to jail, which was true if you were caught and lived long enough to feel the effects.

So, it should come as no surprise if I told you all teachers should be drug-free. But is that the case? Unfortunately not. There just so happens to be more teachers on drugs than you might think, not including myself. Do they get away with it? Yes, way too often. But are they really getting away with it? Not so much.

A teacher's job can be very tiring, but not on the body—on the mind, the one thing that drugs attack firsthand. There is no doubt about it, the brain will always work longer and harder than the body, and this is dominant for teachers.

So, mental health is of most importance for an educator. Drugs effect people's mental health in so many negative ways, and we'd run out of paper if we made an attempt to find all the scientific research just to add them to this book. Just the fundamental problems alone should be enough to make you consider a drug-free life. Most schools are already drug-free, even to the point of banning tobacco products, so no cigarette breaks. This should not be devastating for anyone, being that they are indirectly adding days to your life; the less you smoke, the more you live.

So, what are the fundamental problems that a person might have while under the influence or after?

You remember in Part 1 when we talked about waking up in a good mood and starting your day off right? Well, that isn't going to happen.

Fundamental problem number one is some teachers are working through the day to get to the high. Most of the teachers I come into contact with are in a fairly good mood, but there are those who are a bit strange—the ones who don't really want to talk about the kids ever and always zoning out when you are talking to them. There is clearly something else on their mind. You talk to them long enough, you'll be sure to find out. Let me make it clear that I do understand some are tired and may not like their job, but like I said earlier, there are those who are just strange.

For instance, I can remember being on the playground with the children and watching them as they go. These were fourth graders. The fourth-grade teachers were all sitting in an exclusive area for teachers only, discussing private matters that should only be talked about at home—but I digress. I just so happened to be talking to one of the male educators, and we began our conversation about vacations, which led to talk about the many variables involved with planning a vacation, but as I said you'll be sure to find out if you talk to someone long enough. It wasn't long before he was telling me about his smoking and drinking habits on the beach and, to my surprise, also on a daily basis. This was very disappointing to me but not my life. He was a great teacher with lots of personality, but he hated his job as an educator, which led to his departure.

I've also had the privilege of working with many other teachers that claimed to smoke weed every day after school. I'm not saying all of this to put anyone out there, but we have a serious problem with our students already as it relates to drugs. We cannot lose the teachers, as well. There needs to be some type of self-respect for the career path that you are going on. At the least, wait until summer.

To my knowledge, drugs are extremely misleading. They tell you of a time where you were having fun, and you need them to continue that fun. And as we all can attest to, anything is better than work, even cutting grass with a push mower in Georgia on a hot and humid day in July. Drugs are just what you have decided to do in your time outside of work, and if you have picked up that habit, you are only going to drive yourself to a state of madness trying to gain that unattainable bliss. You will always be happier outside of work, but if you become attached to something as simple as weed or pills, it will start to consume other parts of your life, and slowly but surely it will take precedence over everything in your life, even your family.

I grew up in a neighborhood where I watched drug addicts and their habits; I watched fights over drugs and even arrests. Of course, at times, the drugs they were using were much stronger than those many teachers use for recreation, but all it takes sometimes is a gateway. While growing up in this environment, I quickly learned that drugs were something that I wanted no part of. It was like every time I saw someone on drugs, I only saw the negatives and none of the positives. To this day, I have never done one single drug in my life, and I do not plan on consuming any, no time soon.

It is not a suitable way to find relief from your daily struggles. As an educator, you need more practical ways of bliss that you won't be restrained from while working. A more drug-free outlet is, in my suggestion, something you can do even while at work, and, if possible, this way should dramatically change your whole mental health in the process.

In 2022, teachers are under the influence of antidepressants and other prescribed medications. Teachers are struggling more than ever with their personal mental health. The issue is not the fact that teachers have problems and are overwhelmed; the problem is how they might choose to deal with the issues. I live a drug-free life because I want to live a life of complete emotional control. I need to be in control of my feelings to notice the feelings of the children that I'm working with.

There are schools all over the world, and I am sure that each and every one would prefer that you are drug-free. When teachers are drug-free, they are better for their students. Living a drug-free lifestyle is a choice you must make as a teacher because, at this point, there is too much at stake. There are students shooting schools, committing suicide, raping one another, and impregnating each other during teenage years. The students are too weak as it already is; they can no longer be surrounded by weak teachers, as well. We must stop making excuses about what we feel we are incapable to do as educators.

If you are one of those teachers that have had moments where you felt like you needed something to smoke or drink or you were going to nut up, that's okay. The problem comes when you act upon this impulse and think that this is the one thing that you need to feel better. When you hinge your entire happiness and clarity on this, it becomes a slippery slope to cope. You have to be strong for the students because, at this point, the teachers are the last resort to a dying generation.

Questions for Self-Reflection

1. Are you currently on any medication that keeps you stable during the day?

____

____

____

____

____

2. Are you currently addicted to any drugs?

____

____

____

____

____

3. How would you rate your control over your mental health on a scale of one to ten (one being no control, ten being excellent)?

____

____

____

____

____

4. Are you in control of your thoughts and actions a majority of the day?

____

____

____

____

____

Part 3

What the Students Need from You . . .

INTRODUCTION

Congratulations! You have made it to the last portion of the book. In this part of the book, we will be discussing what the children need from you. There is no doubt that most of the things our children need the most, we cannot provide. Over the years, I have been around children in heartbreaking situations. I have seen children go through things that a child should never have to go through. It breaks my heart to sit here and even think about what I have seen. To me, in this world full of money and opportunity, a child should not have to suffer. But we truly live in a broken world where children are neglected, but adults act like children are praised.

My passions for childcare have always gotten stronger and stronger over the years, and now all I seek to do is provide an experience to the children like no other. I draw strength because I've been that person who sits at the hospital with a child for multiple hours per day waiting for a foster parent to arrive.

I've been that person who separates three siblings into three separate foster homes in one day from one another and watch them cry helplessly because all they want to do is stay with one another. Is that so much to ask? I've seen parents arrested for drug possession, and kids trapped in the system due to it. I've watched kids walk home from a church to a home with no roof. I've worked closely with kids who went on to commit murder, and others that were murdered. I've worked with rape victims and those who suffered from child molestation. The list goes on and on.

I am beyond tired of what I see this world doing to our children. It is time for it to end and a new thing to begin. The kids have been waiting for someone that they can trust and someone who gets it. They have been waiting for that person who is going to bring them out of that mental darkness. They have been seeking and searching for the one who will put an end to the warfare going on in their head and bring them to a place of peace. They are excited to know that help is on the way; they are excited to see that it's right around the corner, and they have hope that it won't take long.

So, who might that person be that they wait so patiently for? You!

It is time for you to finish strong. Get this in your head: YOU ARE ALL THEY HAVE, BUT YOU ARE ALL THEY NEED.

We are going to explore the final steps to becoming the greatest teacher of all time, and when you are done, students will be desiring to be in your class. This part is going to teach you what your students need from you more than anything. You will learn everything that I know, including that which frees me from the mental stress of caring so much.

These kids need us.

Let's imagine for a second that every teacher that ever taught got this in their head. Let's imagine a world where every teacher was competing to become the greatest teacher a child has ever had. How different would the school be if every teacher were just as amazing as Ms. Frizzle from *The Magic School Bus*? The crazy part is that it's not that hard to accomplish; most teachers just intentionally choose not to do it.

The average student goes to school for fourteen years, if they decide not to go to college. This means a student will meet multiple teachers over the course of fourteen years, and if every one of those teachers put in 100 percent, regardless of how they might feel, we'd never have to worry about students again!

So, let's get into what the kids need and can only get from teachers.

To Be Aware

Aware can be defined as knowledge or perception of a situation or fact. Being aware means everything. It controls the flow, and no matter what you are trying to teach, it is a part of having control. The environment is yours, and you control the seasons and nature of what goes on. You are your own boss and practically God in that room. Everything is on you—how the kids feel, how they react to one another, how they treat your things, and how they treat you. You control the weather, and even if storms come into that very classroom, you cannot be afraid to embrace them because the storms always bring more awareness.

I'm reminded of this short story that I read in a book called *Mondays with My Old Pastor* that goes like this:

> It is said that one day there was a peasant who asked God if he could rule over nature so that it could produce better crops for him. And God granted him his wish! From that moment on, when the peasant wanted a light rain, it happened; when he asked for sunshine, the celestial king of the sky shone in all its splendor; if he needed water, it rained harder.
>
> But when the time of harvest came, his surprise and shock were great, because it was a complete failure. Upset and angry, he asked God why the experience had

> ended that way. Why did the crop turn out bad, since he asked for what he thought was the perfect weather?
>
> God answered him, "You asked for what you wanted, but in reality that was not what you needed. You never asked for a storm, and those are necessary to cleanse the sowing of the seed, to scare away the birds and animals that destroy it, and to purify it from pestilences that are very destructive."

The moral that I took from the story was, storms will make you aware of things that you never knew existed before. But as a teacher you feel like it is your job to avoid storms, which I completely understand.

Jordan Peterson said in his book *12 Rules for Life*, "A hurricane is an act of God. But failure to prepare, when the necessity for preparation is well known—that's sin." Most times, until you allow a student to explode, you never get to know the real them and what might be really going on at home. Kids will hold it in and teachers will keep it dormant. I say let it out. As soon as you understand the issue, you will know the right approach to take. As a teacher, you can never prepare perfectly for everything, but what you can do is allow behavior infractions.

It is not your job to have a perfect classroom, but it's nice to be aware of when the necessary changes might need to be made. You are the one who has to deal with it, and the key to your magic will be complete and total awareness, like *The Art of War*. Let's face it, you cannot be truly effective if you are not aware.

For example, there is a child in your class that is giving you so many signals that he or she is bored. They began with small signals like throwing things in the trash or sharpening pencils just to allow time to pass a little more. They arrive back to their seat and begin to talk and whisper to their fellow classmates. Next, maybe they ask to go use the restroom, and once they have asked to go and use the restroom, generally speaking, they are no longer engaged with the lesson.

So, where was the most effective place to intervene as an instructor? Because if you have allowed it to go this far, there is no coming back for that student on this day.

If you are a teacher that is aware, then your answer to the question might have been when they began getting out of their seat, and that would be partially correct. However, you lost them before they decided to start getting up, so the most effective place to intervene was when you were creating your lesson plans. You should know what would bore your students to death and what will entertain them and keep them on their toes. As their primary instructor you should be aware enough to keep them on their toes and have them excited about learning every day.

Basically, knowing what makes your students tick is a part of your job, and if you do not know your students down to a science, you are not doing it right.

Let's take a closer look at what it means to really be aware, because in a school setting full of developing teens and kids with genius-status neuropath ways being created, you can hardly get anything past them. And in today's society, being extremely emotionally charged with little to no control over how they react, you need to stay on your Ps and Qs. This is more than a daily job; this is a chemistry lab full of deadly chemicals.

Imagine there is a tree, and leaves have fallen around that tree. If I then ask you how those leaves got there, with your knowledge of season change and the environment, you can come up with a good answer based on what you know in general. So, let's assume you came up with the answer: it's fall, a light breeze, maybe even a little rain, all caused the leaves to fall to the ground. Now, the knowledge you have come up with is from past experience. You can go no further with your answer than pulling from the past, which is knowledge acquired, and it is very helpful.

However, the only way you can tell me what truly happened in order for us to get to the bottom of it, you would have had to be there. In other words, you would have to have had experienced the leaves falling, because who's to say it wasn't a leaf blower, an animal, or even a storm that made all this come about?

The point that I am getting at is, go to college as long as you think you need to, but knowledge will never trump experience, which is awareness in a nutshell. As an educator, you have to be on top of every situation because you have all the answers and your students need them to get through the day peacefully. The children need you to be aware so you can help them weather their own storms, because we all know that when you are working with children that have storms often, you should also know what it takes for them to get there.

Educators have to pay attention so well that they know their every move and what is normal and abnormal for each student. This makes you extremely effective. It's almost like chess: If you stay enough moves ahead of your opponent, you can control most of the game, and there is nothing more rewarding than winning a flawless victory.

Awareness in the classroom also shows kids that you do not play and they will not get away with anything, and kids need that. Most kids these days do not have anyone like that in their life: people holding them accountable to a T. Their own parents may not be aware of what they do day in and day out, but you have to be, for the most part.

This is going to dramatically change the dynamics of your classroom. When I am working with a group of students, I pay close attention to each and every one of their moves and how they are reacting to the lesson that I am teaching. That way, if I feel as though a few of them are getting bored, I might take a stretch break or may even stop for the day, but at no point am I going to allow them to gain any type of control, not even over their own restroom breaks.

Kids need to feel as if you have their undivided and full attention. You must never divert your attention to anything else during instructional time. Once you break contact, you lose control, and everything can go from good to bad very quickly.

If you are the type that gives busywork, you have no control—you might think it's control, but it's not. How can you know who is working to their full potential and who is not? I see so many children finesse busywork! Again, that's where they are gaining a little control and building their own work habits. They need you to show them how hard they need to work and not allow them to choose on their own. If you are going to give them busywork, make sure you are constantly walking around and making sure everyone is working at a pace that you know they are capable of. Do not—and I repeat *do not*—go to your desk and check emails or browse the internet, send text messages, because in all these things you are losing your awareness and, ultimately, your control.

Know who is participating and who is not during your lecture time, and I mean know enough to get them involved in some way. This alone will help you to understand who is getting it and who is not.

If you have a long history with students, like me, you will already know how to motivate even the shy ones to get involved. You should never have to ask your students to participate if you have made your lecture clear enough for them to understand. They'll be motivated to participate because knowing something or understanding something gives them a sense of empowerment, and they need that.

Kids often tend to do things that may not always make sense, and other students will do things that never make sense. When you are observing your classroom as a whole, one question you need to ask yourself at all times is, *What are they doing and why are they doing it?* This will not only keep you safe, but it will also keep the other students safe. By asking this question, you are always trying to get to the bottom of what's going on in the surrounding area. Unconsciously, you are preparing for that hurricane that may or may not happen.

Kids are always up to something, or in a more politically correct way, they are always trying to find ways to stimulate their brain, and with you being aware of this, you can control the how. They may not enjoy the task you may give them in order for them to get that stimulation, but once it becomes a habit, they will desire it.

Going deeper into that, your goal as an educator is to educate them with all the time you have, meaning you should seek to make every experience a learning one for them. They will grow to enjoy it.

I'm sure most of you are saying to yourself, *This is nothing new. I do all this and more*. And that is great, but for those of you who are not, I have a few more nuggets.

Watching how your students enter the class is a major part of your awareness, and this will tell the tale if you are not aware of how they feel going in. Some kids are going to enter your classroom excited and ready to learn, but there are also going to be those who enter disconnected with a chip on their shoulders. Relatively, you have about ten minutes to get every child acclimated and on the same page. Your goal upon their entrance is to make sure all of them are connected and on the same page, ready to learn.

If you think you can teach with a few of them disconnected, you are sadly mistaken. All children have the same potential to learn; some just need a little help catching up with the others at times. Make sure you take the proper amount of time you need so that they are able to be on the same page with you and the other students.

Lastly, you must stay engaged with the children at all times. It is rare that you get all of the children on the same page, meaning it is no easy task. But if you just so happen to do it, keep them there as long as possible, even if it means diverting from the lesson a little. Joint attention is extremely good for them, and they need to learn to enjoy it. Being engaged with the students is how you are going to be able to stay aware.

Some of the best teachers that any of us have ever had were the ones who were always engaged with us. I'm not talking about the ones who sat and talked to us, but the ones who entertained our conversations. Somehow they knew that this was better than them teaching us what they wanted us to know because, at that moment, we were growing all at the same time.

As an educator, there are so many golden moments and if you are not aware, you will miss out on all of the rewards that come with teaching. Being there in the present time with the students is pivotal to their growth—they need it. You have to be there with them in mind, body, and spirit, helping them react to bullies the proper way and teaching them how they should respond to rude comments, showing them how to have a conversation and stay on topic so that everyone gets a turn to speak.

These are the things that you will not have time to actively teach them, so you have to be aware enough and engaged enough to know when the appropriate time arises. They need someone to be aware when someone is really bothering them and when they are not. They need to know you are not just there, but you are really there with them, involved and interested in their lives and well-being, not because you get paid for it, but because they mean something to you.

Questions for Self-Reflection

1. Are you aware of what goes on in your classroom 100 percent of the time? If so, write a time where you caught something going on that could have ended badly. If not, write of a time where you were caught off guard.

____

____

____

____

____

2. Do you allow storms in your classroom? Yes or no.

3. When a child is no longer engaged with the lesson, where do you notice the first social cue?

____

____

____

____

____

4. Do you hold your students accountable for each and every thing? Yes or no.

5. Are you always aware of how every child enters your classroom? If so, what strategy do you use to greet them at the door?

____

____

____

____

____

Consistency

Consistency is single-handedly the most important aspect of your classroom. This will allow the kids to understand more about the inner workings of your classroom, how you react to missing work, how you allow them to work, and how much they will get away with. Consistency sets up boundaries for the students to work within, and if there is not much room or too much room, consistency will tell the difference. Consistency is very useful. The more you practice consistency, the better. Consistency is law and order.

No matter who you are, if you are human, chances are you will always work better if someone has set boundaries for you to work within. When there are laws set before a class of students, this helps them not only manage their own expectations, but also helps you to manage their expectations. Giving a child or teenager boundaries, and being consistent on the enforcement of said boundaries, allows them to grow within the space you have provided.

For example, when children enter a class where I am the conductor, my first goal is to help them understand my rules and why I have them. Once they understand my rules and they have them memorized, we can begin to move forward into the lesson. This gives the law within our small society, and if anyone breaks the laws, I will enforce some type of punishment.

This is effective because this allows me to know what I need for them to do moving forward, and I can stop when they are not following my expectation. Unexpected behaviors will not be tolerated, and when they understand that, they can learn a lot more.

Now, there will be those who intentionally break your laws, and you have to be consistent and fair with your consequences. For instance, if one kids talks all the time and gets the same punishment as one who never talks yet gets caught for the first time, that is not fair. The consistent thing to do is to make sure whatever you do as a punishment, it persuades the other students to not make the same mistake. Kids have an amazing way of noticing when things are unfair; even the least bit of unfairness will change the dynamic of your class, and you may lose the respect of most of them for good.

Keeping the respect of your students is a big part of why you should be consistent in everything you do in your class. Consistency with the following is mandatory: engaging them, emotions, lectures, work habits, homework, and punishments, etc. What you do and how you act daily needs to be controlled to some degree.

Just imagine the inconsistent lives they come from. Have you ever noticed how much a kid respects a parent that is never at home? Or how much they respect a parent that's in a good mood some of the time and a bad mood at other times? If you become mentally unstable for even a day, it is best that you do not show up to work. This helps you maintain your balance with the students.

How you treat them needs to depend on them. The ball needs to constantly be in their court so they receive ample opportunities to work on themselves. How often is it that children meet a brick wall that will not be moved and they have to figure out what to do? It is rare, but it is also a need. If they will not receive this type of structure at home, then we are forced to introduce it in the schools. Society will not teach them, it will only punish them. We are always trying to give them the answers to their problems and tell them what they need to do. They need to figure it out for their own empowerment. Be consistent with follow-up answers in the form of probing questions because that's where their empowerment will come in.

There is an equation I teach those who are thinking of working with children in the future: C + C = C. Being casual plus consistent will equal control.

The **casual** part is the most questionable to most because it's almost a contradiction. However, when I say *casual,* I mean *relaxed in your tone,* as if you know the full outcome of what is going to happen. You need to be casual because it shows them that what was said will not be taken personally, and in the end, how they act only affects their day and not yours. You will never see a scientist arguing at the particles she or he is manipulating. How the particles react and the full outcome are in her or his control.

This is one way to assert your power over them, and be sure to do it consistently. There are no adults that should ever be caught arguing with a child; it's embarrassing. Don't humiliate yourself. From a distance, you will only look like a fool.

Of course, **consistency** is the next part of the equation, being the root of all good classrooms. Ninety-nine out of the one hundred questions that teachers have asked me, consistency has been the root of the problem.

Are you being consistent? If you have a student that has a problem turning in their work, do you consistently give out work and stay on them about turning it in? If you have a problem with a student talking while you are teaching, do you consistently give a consequence to their action and stay on them all of the time? Consistency works all across the board—newborns, pets, millionaires, even the military. It's the key to any successful environment. If you are failing at being consistent, then you are failing at gaining control.

Control—the desired outcome we are all seeking. To gain control of anything, you need a plan that you can trust enough to work, and do not deviate from that plan until you see the results you are looking for. Our job as educators is to make a safe learning environment for students, a place where they are comfortable showing their learning capabilities and gifts. Once you gain control, you can begin to control their expectations and yours, as well, as stated earlier.

Your expectation for your students is at your discretion. It can be a goal as high as every student in your class to pass with an A, nothing less of an A. After you know what you are expecting from them, you are able to let them know what they need to do to gain that. The mistake most educators make is we constantly fall into not letting them know their part in your class, and that gives them lots of room to exploit the unsaid.

Make sure you make it crystal clear what you expect from them and allow them to see how you all will achieve it together, and be consistent with whatever is working until you gain the outcome of a class full of A students.

Be unmovable, because your desired goal is bigger than anything else during the year. Even if you lose hope in your plan, do not move from the standards that you have set before them. The big picture of a student that is expected to make an A is a healthy work habit with self-discipline, and that is what you are trying to create—something that they will not only need, but also use for a lifetime.

The most important advice I'd give you is when cultivating the atmosphere in your class, make it as narrow as possible. Too much space gives them a lot of room to exploit and causes you to be on your toes all the time. A child will no longer become a product of the environment you created; you are now at the will of an environment they control.

For example, if you are purchasing a house, you set a law for yourself of a certain price that you are willing to pay, and you don't plan to go past this price mark. This will keep you in check and in control of what you decide to look at. If you don't set a price, you are at the risk of spending more than you have to offer and, even worse, your false expectation for reality letting you down. Consistency is law and law is order.

Now, don't get me wrong—this all may sound easy, but it is not! There are many battles you will have to face to get to the point you want to be at. This generation of kids does not allow anything, even the smallest of things, to come easy. Before you can even attempt to speak to a child sternly, you have to cultivate a relationship. They will never care what you think unless they know that you care. Once a relationship has been established, then you can begin to be consistent with how you operate in it.

Questions for Self-Reflection

1. Do you have law and order in your classroom?

2. What is C + C = C?

3. What is your job as an educator?

4. Should the expectations be wide or narrow? Explain why.

FORGIVENESS

Forgiving is when one does not take anything personal. Now, this is not the correct way to define forgiveness; it is just my way when working with children.

How can anyone take anything that comes out of a child's mouth seriously? For the most part, everything they say is based on how they feel. Most kids in my daily encounters act without thinking, and half the time I get a good laugh out of the whole thing.

If I took everything a child did to me, at me, or told me personally, I would not be writing a book about how to connect with them better; I'd be writing about addiction. Every now and again I hear people say, "These people will drive you to drink," and I'm a little curious, at times, of the first individual to coin that saying. Then I think of teachers, because if you take things personal easily, these kids will drive you to drink (if you're not already doing so).

The key to any wonderful, happy environment full of potential is based on how quick the people in that place are to forgive. When you are in a place where you know you are going to be forgiven, the workload is much easier.

In this world, kids are given one chance, even if they are lacking in the understanding. So often they are verbally abused by peers and the adult in their life for making an honest mistake.

They need more people in their life who will talk to them, even when they have been extremely rude, and they need people who will easily clean the slate for the next day.

Every time I tell an adult that a child I worked with hit me, or spit on me, or cursed at me, they all say the same thing: "If I were you I would have . . ." And what they would have done is usually an act of violence, which is never the answer.

Forgiving your students helps them overcome fear. **Fear** is a driving force of how a lot of children react, and this affects their grades, attitudes, and classroom habits. If you have ever seen a report card of a student that you know is trying their best yet they are still failing, it's likely they have been placed with an unforgiving teacher. I'll be the first to say dogs do not prefer to eat paper, so if the student is constantly missing work, this is something that needs to be addressed. However, if they are doing the work and just not passing it and failing tests, then that is also something that needs to be talked about with the right words.

Educators, you have to understand that some of your students come from homes with uneducated parents and no internet to browse—at least, that was the home I came from.

I was a good student, growing up quiet, respectful, and interested in learning. But there were a few teachers in my life that cared nothing about that and were very unforgiving when it came to my grades. I would do the work; I just didn't always make the best grade on my work. I got to the point where I feared even turning in my work or even trying on tests, and that directly showed on my progress reports. My parents were not concerned enough for me to make all A's, but they were enough to make sure I was doing what I needed to do to pass. My dad made sure I feared him more than I feared not turning in my work.

My teacher began to notice my father was willing to step in and do what he needed to do to make sure I did the work. However, I still needed help. Because the teacher understood a deeper dynamic behind the relationship of my work ethic and intelligence, it was easy for them to forgive and forget, and help me as much as they could. Going forward, I was able to do better because my teacher was more forgiving toward my work.

Failing forward is learned through how often you are or have been forgiven. Teachers that forgive their students are planting seeds that will harvest the rest of each child's life and help them a lot along the way. There are so many students that do not receive forgiveness because of race, status, or history, and because of this, they will hardly ever find the opportunity to change. Fear is so dominating because it's the only emotion they have been taught to notice, so when they experience it, they know it. They begin to learn ways to cope with the fear, and most of the time, it is through escape.

And how does anyone escape? By avoiding. We can combat this by showing the child that we are there to help and there is no need for them to fear us or fear turning in the work we ask them to.

Students need to know that teachers have their backs 100 percent, and if they fail, it is because they did not try. If a teacher is not as forgiving as they should be, this generally will affect the child's attitude and will affect the teacher in the long run.

Kids can tell when the adult in the room is being real and also when they are attempting to hide their fakeness. So, it serves you best to be authentic. Building that authentic relationship comes with forgiving. We are able to slowly break walls down that separate us from them through how much we are forgiving them. Even if you do not know a kid all that well, you can forgive them. Actually, it is much easier to forgive a person you do not know that well.

There was I book I read that narrated an excellent example of how we should forgive. It spoke of a man's relationship with a pet, such as a dog.

My dog and I have a typical relationship, but honestly I make it very hard on my dog at times. I'm not the most energetic when it comes to having pets; I'm more of a people person. But be that as it may, I come home from work at times so tired and in need of some "me time," but as soon as I walk in the door, there is my dog, Apollo, there to greet me, because all day he has been waiting for some "us time."

Every day it's the same process, and I push him away every time. Yet, he is persistent in attempting to communicate to me that he wants to play, and I'm persistent in showing that I do not.

You would think that by now my dog would get the picture and just leave me alone when I walk in the door, but he doesn't. Every day he just does the same thing. But there is one thing that he does during the whole process: He goes and lays down in an area where he can directly just look at me, and he waits. When I finally get the time and space that I was needed, he jumps up ready to play again and as happy as ever.

In that situation, we should be like the dog. Some days the kids are going to come into the classroom and they are just not going to be in the mood. When we notice that, we need to forgive them and allow them to have the space they need to cope. When they are ready to come back to earth, we should not take that opportunity to throw it back up in their face and say, "Now I need some space." We need to be thoughtful and forgiving.

There are a few other times where we can practice being forgiving, as well, such as when they ask a question that you would consider stupid, for the lack of better words. Most adults say that there is no such thing as a stupid question, but I beg to differ. Sometimes it seems as if some of our students intentionally ask some of the stupidest questions, but that is still not an excuse to call them out on it. Even when they ask a question that you know you have answered, try to forgive them and act as if the question was just asked for the first time.

Remember, if they are engaged or trying to be, you will have questions, and if they are engaged, that is good enough, even at the expense of a few not-so-very-smart questions. This will allow them to continue to have confidence when it comes to asking questions.

Another act of forgiveness is being excited even when they

are not excited. This will show them that even on their bad days, you will remain unaffected. There is nothing worse than a teacher whose moods depend on their students. They are kids; at times they won't be excited. First of all, it is school. Many kids don't get excited about school anymore. And second, they want to be on their phones. So, being excited shows them that there is no other place in the world that you would rather be than there with them, and eventually they will join you in your excitement.

This one is going to sound crazy: forgive them even when they break the laws of your classroom. Notice I said *forgive them*, and yes, you have to forget in order to forgive, but also keep the standards in the process. They will break your laws many times, over and over again. But this will be the ultimate test to see if you truly are ready to begin to forgive them.

So, in a nutshell, kids need a space where they know they are able to be free to an extent.

It's no mistake that art, physical education, and music have some of the most fun and laid-back teachers there are in a school; it's because they have different expectations than you do, and they don't have to have much control. They are flexible to be as forgiving as they need to be to their students. But it's different for you, and just because it is different does not mean it can't be as fruitful. Once you have set your boundaries and gain their respect, they will enjoy your class because of how you have set the standard. Adding forgiveness will only give your class more juice in the long term.

QUESTIONS FOR SELF-REFLECTION

1. When working with children, is it ever a good time to take anything they say personally?

2. What is the driving force of negative behaviors in a student?

3. How can you better establish a forgiving relationship with your students?

4. How can you practice to enhance your excitement?

PATIENCE

Patience is being able to accept or tolerate delay, problems, or suffering without becoming annoyed or anxious. Patience—do children even know what this is? Do they notice when someone is giving them the benefit of the doubt, and can they even spell this word?

I personally think not, because they are not even patient themselves, so how can they appreciate something they have never seen?

When you are patient with a child, you are interested in their general well-being, and *this* they will notice without a problem. We have to be patient for these simple reasons: learning delays, home life, lack of understanding, the nature of our job . . . and we are getting paid!

There is not one kid on this earth that thinks the same and at the same pace as another; all of them think differently. With that being said, the proper way of saying this is each child will have a different learning curve.

A learning curve is the rate of a person's progress in gaining experience or learning a new skill. If you are a teacher, chances are you already are aware of this (or you definitely should be). When a teacher understands a child's learning curve, this will allow them to seek a deeper understanding and strategically plan a way to educate the student—not to mention how much this will help a teacher when she or he is struggling to have patience.

Some children will learn very fast and others will learn extremely slowly, and it is your job to get them to the same outcome in the desired time, which is an entire school year. The notion of teaching A students to be on the same page as C students might sound insane when said and looked at in that way, but that truly is the job. When you allow yourself to accept that and not do what most teachers do—complain—then you will better understand what it will take to get it done. Your patience will only kick in after this is accepted. Don't get me wrong, it is a much easier task when said rather than done, like herding cats to a puddle.

Moving on to another note, if I explained something to you for the first time, you would probably have a hard time understanding it. Even if I was capable of understanding it down to a T myself, you may still be lacking in details for you to learn what it is I am trying to teach. When it comes to teaching, we have to give the children as much time and help as they need to gain the understanding that they will need for the future.

Our understanding and their lack thereof needs to meet somewhere in the middle. How well they will understand will depend on how long we are willing to be patient, because, as I said, we all have different learning curves. Some of the time you might think you are being clear enough for even a blind and deaf person to understand, but they still may not understand themselves.

So, how can we better judge when we are being clear enough to continue or when we need to dumb it down a little?

The questions they ask will be specific if they understand, and they will be as broad as anything you'd ever seen before if they are not understanding—like, "What did you say?" versus "What did you mean when you said . . . ?" Blah, blah, blah. The latter is an indication that they are somewhat getting the information that you are putting out, but if they ask the first question, be prepared to stop what you are doing and start over. Starting over may be reoccurring most of the year, but this might be what it takes for that child to one day have that desired breakthrough.

One thing that will also be a deciding factor on how well and fast a child is able to learn is home life. I have said this many times in this book, and I'll say it more before we are done: the home life is the most important factor you are up against. We all have been there in this job where there is one kid that you just worry about so much and wish you could take them home, but that will never happen. Well, maybe some of the time it will happen, but it's not a practical way of looking at your job at hand, because no matter the circumstances, it truly is only your job to educate them.

By doing so, you will have given them more than they will ever need, and as long as they continue to use the education, it will take them further than you'll ever know. But until then, let's get back to home life and what to do in the process.

One thing that I have always kept in mind as I've worked with so many kids is, I win no matter what. Kids sometimes come to our environment from broken places, which means they lose majority of the time. Maybe they have no food or clean shelter, maybe no proper clothing to wear on a normal school day. Sleeping arrangements may not be up to par. We don't know, but what do we know?

The amount of emotional trauma they are dealing with is unfathomable, and we will never understand the homes they come from. We need to be patient with these little ones (and sometimes these big ones), otherwise they will never have a place where they can win and be happy.

When we clock out and go home, we win, or at least we should win. If our lives were to be compared to just a few of our students, we would see that there would be a dramatically different outlook on our world versus theirs. They need these wins, we don't, so why not create an environment that they can be excited about coming to for once, especially if you are teaching in the inner-city or low-income areas of the United States?

When I was doing youth ministry, I was in an area that was extremely dangerous and poor (it seems violent acts become normal when other humans have a hard time getting their basic needs met). I had just got done teaching a message one Sunday and decided to take some kids from the youth department home. I was so excited about them being able to ride in my new clean car, which at the time was a 2016 midsize sedan. As I drove, I showed them all the cool stuff about the car and what I kept in it. Me being naïve as I was at the time, I didn't realize when I might have been coming off as braggy to them (that day, I also had $700 from my recent tax return that I was keeping in my car).

I dropped them off and proceeded home, and on the way, my wife and I talked about how sweet they were and how bad we felt about their home life. I based my messages around having hope in God for the future during that week.

I got to church excited to see them and preach the message I had come up with, and as I looked into my small crowd of youth, they were not there. This made me a little sad because I thought I'd scared them off or made them feel differently about me.

When church was over and we were in the back talking with the adults, a man came over to me and said, "Do you drive the green car?" to which my answer was yes. He then told me that it had been broken into. I went outside to check, and the driver-side window was shattered. I checked for my belongings, and sure enough, the money that I'd kept in the middle console was gone and some other things were, too. I made a choice then and there to not get upset about it and not let it bother me. My wife was different because she had left her purse inside, and her things were gone, too.

The biggest coincidence was the fact that we never saw those kids again that we'd taken home the week before, and we continued to work at that church for another two years and take kids home all the time. Now, I'm not going to sit here and say those kids did it or didn't do it; this is not about that. We have to remember some things that are way left for us might be right for them. Hunger will drive a person either mad or willing to do anything.

Home life is the leading cause for lack of education, and if we are not patient enough, we will see record numbers of kids dropping out of schools more often than not. Whoever broke into my car will regret it, and it may only be for that day or the rest of their life. It will eat them up on the inside, but when it comes down to life or death, I don't blame them—I would have done the exact same thing given the circumstances.

When being in any field of academia, most of our most daunting questions will come directly from the students. There is this one question that comes often from the students, but also (and mostly) the adults: "What were you thinking when you decided to teach?"

Surely you were not thinking money, power, and respect, because in your first year of teaching, your student loans will take your money, the paper work takes your power, and the kids eat your respect for breakfast and poop it out by lunch. So, what were the thoughts of most of us that decided to go into teaching for a living (or a dying—whichever you want to call it)?

I believe, given no credit to popular belief, that in some way, shape, or form, we all loved working or being around children. That has to be the deciding factor. I think the environment was what motivated us the most. There are those who went in for security, such as retirement, and others because it was such an easy degree.

But if you are like me at all, you went for the sheer joy of being around children. Their fun, upbeat energy and outlook on life was enough to draw me. They do not let anything bother them for longer than twenty minutes. What I mean is that if there is something that just looks better than their current situation they are in, they are fearless when it comes to making decisions. Though they also make emotional decisions, they know how to do it without allowing it to eat them up on the inside, and sometimes that rubs off on us.

So, since we are already in this field, we have to be patient because it is a part of our job description. We chose this career, no matter *how* we chose it. We are not forced to go into this job every day; we have enough sense to quit something that we do not like. We also have the power to manifest a different lifestyle if that is also what we choose to do. But for those of us who are into teaching for the long haul, we must be patient.

The kids do not get to choose if they want to be educated or not; they are here because they have to be. When the students are occupying the same space as you, it is a partnership. You want to be there and they have to be there, so make the best of it. Your life was chosen—where you went to get your degree, and who you married, and where you decided to live, and the paycheck you decided to agree to. You control the whole narrative, but is this the same for them? Did they choose to be born of their parents, or live in the country, state, or city that they do? What about what they wanted to wear? Because I'm sure if they had it their way, what they wear would be much more expensive. And when it comes to them being there, if they had it their way at all, they would definitely not be at school . . . but you are!

So it is your duty to be as patient as you can be, but being patient to a point is the key. We cannot allow them to just run the classroom and do what they want to do. Though some of us may not mind letting the kids run the classroom, this just cannot and should not happen due to the fact that it is our job to teach, and we are getting paid to teach. They must learn for us to keep our jobs.

So often teachers are looking for ways to make the day go by faster so we can get off work and do what we want to do. And those days where the kids are being horrible and we cannot figure out what to do to calm them down, the answer is always right in front of us, and it does not take much to harness it: we have to be patient. If we are, they will not only learn what they need to learn, but in the long run, they will enjoy learning in your classroom. They won't give you a lot of attitude when it comes to getting the work done because they know you are patient and you want what's best for them.

I've had children assist me when I might have been having a hard time motivating one of my students to get busy. In the end, if you are patient, you will be respected.

Questions for Self-Reflection

1. Patience is most important because of what?

2. How does the home life affect the child's school life on a relational level?

3. What were you thinking when you decided to teach?

4. If you could do anything else in the world, would you?

Fun

Fun is enjoyment, amusement, or light-hearted pleasure. With all things considered, why can school not be a fun environment? Does it have to be so serious? Doesn't everyone like to have fun? Why are teachers not trained to teach in a fun way?

There is no excuse on why we cannot have fun while learning; there is not one subject that can't be taught in a fun way. Kids will not get excited about learning if there is not some type of fun going on every day. As educators, we should try to make school a less stressful place for everyone.

Let's make school fun again!

Fun for a kid changes every second of the day. What might have been fun ten years ago may not be fun now. But with the right laws set in place, you can define what *fun* will be in your environment.

When making a fun place for kids to learn, there is a bit of a thin line that has to be drawn; you cannot deviate too far from what you would normally do in a regular day. The goal, ultimately, is for them to have fun while also learning something they need. This may sound very hard to do, but there is hope for us if we look at it from a certain perspective: fun for them is extremely over the top at all times.

There is not one kid on earth, or adult, that has not wanted to go to an extremely fun place over and over at some point in their life. It becomes the most magical place in the world—the smells, the atmosphere, and the people all come together to make it what it is.

What is the secret? Energy and imagination.

So, you won't have to do much to reach their standards, but you have to use your imagination. It has to be something new that they have never seen or done before because kids get bored. Introduce every new topic to them in a fun way. Don't just lecture them about the facts; allow them to see it for the first time in a very fun way. Fun places always keep us on our toes, as they attempt to exceed your expectations every time.

Learning will not be fun unless they are excited about your class in the first place. When you are working with kids and trying to be fun or have fun, one thing you have to keep in mind (and most people forget about this): what might look and sound fun to you may not be fun at all to the kids you are teaching. Be open-minded, work hard, and put yourself in their position. You have a good-enough fun radar to know what would be fun for you and what would not.

So, why are teachers not fun?

Well, I believe it is mostly all the paper work that drags them down. Deep down inside, there are teachers that are desperate to have fun, but they just do not believe they can do something fun and continue to also do their job. Fun only comes when holidays are near, but what I really see on those days are kids babysitting themselves with too much freedom.

When it comes to teaching kids, they also need to learn how to have safe fun because they have no clue. All they know is what their friends show them, and sometimes that involves some of the wrong ingredients. School is a place where we learned how to start a game of hide-and-seek and tag during recess. Also, where we learned to play dodgeball and capture the flag. These games were explained to us and we were told to play them with one another. We learned to love them more than just running around on the playground. We wanted to do something not only organized, but also active. What I can tell you about kids is they don't mind a little order as long as it comes with a little fun, and I think that is fair, being that you will be with them for over seven hours in a day.

So, in all this organized fun, what were the kids really learning to do? Have joint attention. How hard is it nowadays to get kids to do something active together and all be involved in the moving parts of whatever is happening?

We slowly began taking away all the fun out of school—no more dodgeball, and at a certain age we also stopped taking them outside for recess, but we still asked them to be kids.

The biggest problem in our schools today: they are lacking fun. Surely if we want them to act like a child, I think we have to give them more opportunities to be one. They are only growing old and bitter because that is how we are teaching them to be.

Schools are being run like Fortune 500 businesses, with things being said like, "How can we cut costs in this?" and "How can we increase our numbers in that?" We have forgotten the whole purpose that we started out on this journey for. Public schools are getting much worse, and it seems that no one really cares as long as the kids get home without being bullied or judged in any way. And by all means necessary, we maintain ratio. If these standards are being met, then we all can go home somewhat happy.

Over the years as I have been working with children, I have learned certain cues that help me maintain the fun environment. When I see kids doing any of these things then I know for a fact, by my standards, that they are having fun. These cues are laughter, engaged, curiosity, smiles, eye contact, relaxed body language, and always leaving wanting more. You are not going to see all of these signs from every student simultaneously, but there will be students that express these.

Maybe you'll have one or two kids laughing hysterically the entire time—just constant nonstop—and don't get on to them, because this is good for the other kids to hear. Then there will be those who are so into it, they are giving you constant eye contact and ready to answer when a question arises. Some will ask questions out of curiosity and many will smile. When you see most of the cues I have mentioned, you have succeeded at giving the children a fun place to learn.

Kids need fun. If I were to go on strike about the public school system, this would be what my followers and I would yell out: "KIDS NEED FUN!" All of us need time to relax and feel safe, laugh a little, and not take life so seriously all of the time, but kids need it the most. Why would we want to make life boring for them? After all, they will be the ones running the country someday, and the seeds we plant are going to grow.

Fun should always be your number-one goal in your classroom, but also fun should always be in your control.

Questions for Self-Reflection

1. What's the best practice to make a classroom fun in your personal opinion?

2. What examples could we use from fun places we have been to make our classrooms more fun?

3. What age did school stop being fun for you, and why?

4. What body language indicates that a child is having fun?

5. Is there ever a time when fun should take the place of learning?

____

____

____

____

____

ENTHUSIASM

Enthusiasm is having or showing intense and eager enjoyment, interest, or approval. Your bread and butter will always be based on your level of enthusiasm when approaching children on any stage. If you have ever seen a kid show, such as *The Wiggles* or *Barney*, these shows teach us that when working with children, your energy output will be theirs.

When The Wiggles got on stage, they rocked it for as long as they had to, smiling, jumping up and down, and just doing "the most" the entire time. Their ticket sales depended on it. If you are seeking a fun, rewarding day that you can go home and tell your spouse about, then be enthused from beginning to the end.

Kids need us to be excited about the day, and you need to be ready to do whatever it takes for them to learn. I love going into a classroom where the kids expect it to be boring; as soon as they sit, I get loud and very obnoxious. My enthusiasm is through the roof and it wakes them up every time. Some might even say, at times, I go a bit too far but with children. The further, the better. The more excited I am, the more excited they will be. And for those of you who are not excited every day you walk into those classrooms, you do not need to be there.

So often I have heard so many negative things come out of the mouths of teachers, and it's just not right. When someone is being negative in your life, you need to get them as far away as you can, but imagine being a child and having no control of that at all. They can never escape to a place that's good if your attitude is not where it needs to be. There are teachers I know personally who do not need to be working with kids, as we speak, because of their lack of enthusiasm for the job. These are the things that are not going to come with the degree that you earn from college; you have to learn how to do this on your own—for you and the well-being of the kids.

At first, it will feel a bit unusual. I remember dancing in front of children for the first time. It was the weirdest thing! I began by moving slowly for a few moments during the songs we would sing every day, and as I would dance, I would look around, embarrassed of what the other students might be thinking of me at the time. I could never catch them watching me, but there was something inside of me that felt as if they were watching me and laughing behind my back. That was the hardest feeling to get over because at times I could hear them laughing and that made me feel very insecure. I began telling myself that it was okay for them to laugh because it is my job to give them some type of enjoyment. I never stopped dancing. I actually got more and more comfortable with it and more into it until I was completely comfortable.

I have never been a dancer—it is what makes me feel most vulnerable—but when I changed the narrative in my head, I changed the outcome of my dancing. The kids were not laughing at me; they were laughing with me, and this I knew because they were enjoying the music time.

The thoughts that fill our heads will almost never stop, but we can control how we look at them. You cannot let your thoughts keep you from being enthusiastic about your job. Negative thoughts are what keep most people from being happy at work, but finding a way to overcome those thoughts needs to become a daily exercise.

We are social creatures, which means we tend to copy each other when it comes to interaction with one another. For instance, if you stopped and looked around, chances are the people that are interacting with each other look somewhat similar in posture. If one individual has their arms crossed, then it is very likely that the other will also—and it's not magic, it's just how we are built.

While keeping this in mind, and moving forward with your job working with children, your body language will show much of your interest in the lesson. Keep it free-flowing, hand gestures and whatnot. When they notice your behavior, they will translate that through their behavior.

Have you ever watched a televangelist? I say this because The Wiggles may not be your thing, but everyone needs someone to mimic. They are always positive, no matter what they are talking about. Now I'm not assuming that any of it is a lie, but even if they were telling lies, when information is presented with that much energy then there must be something real about it.

Kids are very impressionable, and how you introduce the new topic or game at hand makes all the difference. Fake it until you make it. Be enthusiastic even if you are talking about how paint dries. If you are excited about it, they will be, too.

There are also words and phrases you might want to start using to show a little more of your energy off to the children. I call them "optimistic power phrases." Even in the worst moods, theses phrases come off as positive and energetic. There are certain power words in these phrases that will excite them when said in the right way at certain moments, like the phrase "It's a surprise!" When has this phrase ever let you down? From the moment this is said to you, it takes over you mind.

A good time to use this is when kids are constantly asking, "What are we going to do today?" Instead of saying, "Wait for my directions," or "Class has not yet begun," say, "It's a surprise," and watch their reactions. "Wait and see" is a another one you could use, but this one has to be said in the right tone of voice. If not, it could easily come off as snappy.

When kids are showing up back to school from a break or weekend, there are also things to be said during this time to show enthusiasm. Let's say a child is explaining to you how their weekend went, and you are just listening to them go. When it is your turn to speak, or you have one of those slight pauses, a good thing to infer is "That's so interesting!" Allowing them their time to speak and giving them this type of feedback is so good and so important for them. This will show them, even though you have other students, their life is important to you also.

How many of us connect good customer service with enthusiasm? Maybe all of us! We all respond to positive energy better then negative energy. No one likes an angry bird, so when we are in our classrooms, we must bring good customer service because in the end, we are indeed providing a service, and if the customer is not happy, then ultimately, something about us might need to change a bit.

When I was the manager at the local pizza restaurant, my number-one priority was the customer because if they were happy, they would indeed come back happy and spend more money. Kids are the same: If they are being treated well and they are being taken care of, then they will also come back in a much better mood, of course, but also working harder than they might have before.

Another important lesson I learned from working with customers is that they really are always right. With that being said, children are, half the time, never right, except for when it comes down to your attitude. If they tell you that your lessons and your class are boring or difficult, take their judgment and do what you have to do to change it. Because kids may not always be right, but they are always watching you.

Questions for Self-Reflection

1. How do you define a lack of enthusiasm?

2. What is the most embarrassing thing you have done to entertain your students?

3. Make up a power phrase to make your students excited.

4. How would you rate your enthusiasm on a scale from one to ten (one being none at all and ten being way too much)? Explain what you would rate the perfect amount of enthusiasm as, and why.

Creativity

Creativity relates to or involves the imagination or original ideas, especially in the production of an artistic work.

When building the pyramids of Egypt, they used bricks; in food, we use salt for taste; and on a cake, we prefer to cover it with icing. When it comes to educating children, we must be creative—it is the one thing that will make you go from being a good teacher to a great teacher. The art instructor cannot be the only one in the school that is creative. Every human on earth has the ability to be as creative as they would like to be, but you have to tap into it.

When teachers are not being as creative as they can be, there are two things that come to mind that might be holding them back: Either they are lazy, or they are getting all of their ideas from certain apps.

I have seen the first one more than the second one, unfortunately. Teachers have to work on other things—*that* I understand. You have conferences and IEPs. There is hardly enough time for you to get creative with something as simple as your lunch, so I understand. But being lazy is like a virus—once you begin to do things the easy way, there is hardly any way to get out of doing things any other way. You become accustomed to doing things that way, and in the end, you just become an all-around lazy teacher.

I have seen teachers print things off the computer and didn't even have enough pride to clear it up a bit before they printed it. It's getting bad. Teachers are saying that the paper work is becoming more and more demanding and there is hardly enough time to teach. Somehow we are going to have to figure out a way to work around that notion, because kids are the ones suffering at the end of the day. We have to make a difference, even if it means going on strike about the paper work, because as long as no one speaks up, it will continue to happen and the load will never get lighter, and creativity will cease to exist in the classroom.

We need it in the classroom more now than ever before. Information is out there for everyone, and it is for the taking if you need to use it in any way. Kids need to see someone who is still able to generate an idea.

Tapping into your creativity is not easy; you have to be inspired by something, and finding inspiration at a school is no easy task. When you are inspired, this will kickstart an idea, but it will be up to you to expand on that idea once it begins to come alive in your head.

When you are inspired and able to create, this will affect the kids in so many good ways. They do not want their teachers to do some of the same things that other teachers are doing. Where is the novelty in that? New ideas and lesson plans are the things they need to see firsthand, and lessons that will not only drive you to be more creative, but ones that will also pull the creativity out of your students.

I once worked with this kid that was extremely quiet. She was in the sixth grade and really had a hard time connecting with others. She was great at drawing and painting, but she was so shy that people hardly ever got to see her work. I decided to make it my mission to inspire her to be herself and show her talents to the world. I was painting and drawing more myself, and when I would finish my art, I'd bring it to the school and show the other kids. To her surprise, the other kids' reaction to the artwork was magnanimous—they loved it most of the time and it wasn't even that great. Art was starting to look cool, and she took the opportunity to get some of the spotlight by showing her art, as well.

What I learned from that encounter is all kids want to do great things, but they also want to be looked at as cool. Being too smart or too creative has gotten a bad reputation, but we need to change that. When kids are focused on how they are being seen, they no longer focus on being creative. It seems what is cool has to come from videos or else it is not cool.

With apps and cell phones only, people are more distracted than ever before. The bad part is that their brains are being re-wired. The time that they were creative will no longer be a part of the future for most kids. However, kids are not the only ones who have a brain that is being rewired—teachers are also as distracted as the kids. So, in the end, who will teach them to be creative if teachers are not even creative themselves?

It is impossible to give something that you do not have. If you are an educator, you have to possess creativity yourself. If we took a poll in the school and asked as many teachers as we could find who felt like they were creative, it is my hypothesis that we would find that half of them would not even dare to consider themselves creative at the risk of having to prove it.

Teachers are finding worksheets online, and that is not creative at all because their students are finding the answers to those same worksheets online. Creativity can keep children from cheating on their work and help them to also reach a little closer to their potential. You can always tell how creative a teacher is by how often they change their room and what it looks like. Disorganization has also been associated with creativity, but not with phones. When Einstein was being creative and his entire work area looked a mess, he did not have a phone. We can no longer make a correlation between the two. If you are messy in this day and time, you are just messy.

The only way to get more creative is to be less distracted.

Another way to tell when teachers are not being creative is

their classrooms. There is absolutely, positively no earthly reason we should be walking into a classroom that has walls that remain uncovered. Educators that have been in the game for a while should know that it is your job to create a whole other world. If you teach history, your classroom should be filled with historical things. If science, it should look something like *The Magic School Bus*. If you are too young for that *Magic School Bus* reference, I demand that you go and watch it for yourselves; she will teach you how to teach. But you have to get to work in your classroom—that is your domain; that is how you describe yourself without saying anything. When your classroom is set up in a nice, creative way, it yells to the world, "This is my class and I love what I do."

When we are creative, we are able to do things and create things like never before and expand on an idea in so many other unorthodox ways. The downside to this is that you cannot just wake up one day and say, "I'm going to be creative," but you can say, "Today, I'm going to be *more* creative."

Being creative has to be practiced on the daily, but you'd be surprised how many different opportunities you have to get creative in a day.

Take cooking, for example. How many of us still cook anymore, like really cook from scratch without videos or TV shows that present five-minute cooking tips? Not many of us can get in the kitchen and feel inspired to cook a meal. It requires us to think, and that is something only done in the Stone Age. The funny thing is, it is not the work that drives us not to cook, because when done right, cooking is relatively easy. The simplest of things can convince us not to cook—lack of an unimportant ingredient or even the cleaning process—but the main reason? It's the rigor of coming up with creative elements with what you got. Using what you got in the kitchen is one of the ways the most famous dishes have been created.

Another easy way to work on the creative side of your brain is to play an instrument. Now, you might say, "I have no history in being musical at all," but the point is maybe sometime in your life you were and you could go back to the instrument you were playing then. I saw a poster that once said, "Music opens up parts of the brain that you never knew you had." I wonder what those parts are?

Basically, you have to do something that requires you to be creative. This will make space for creativity in the brain while pushing useless things out of the brain. This we should also be teaching our students.

When we translate and apply this same method to the classroom, using what you got is how great lessons are created. There is no reason for a teacher to go out and spend so much on classroom supplies to teach a lesson. Teaching comes from the heart—all you need is students to teach. You can teach about anything and do it anywhere if you have the heart to teach. If you do not have the heart to teach, then it will be nearly impossible for you to get creative at all.

Questions for Self-Reflection

1. What will make you go from being a good teacher to a great one?

____

____

____

____

____

2. How do you get inspired?

____

____

____

____

____

3. How do you inspire your students?

____

____

____

____

____

4. Are you naturally creative? Explain your answer.

____

____

____

____

____

PASSION

Passion is caused by strong feelings or beliefs toward something of interest. People who work with children have to be passionate about it or you cannot make a real difference.

When passion is flowing out of a person while they are in their environment of choice, it almost is mistaken for anger. It can be scary at times, like a mad scientist working on something that they know is going to change the world.

Passion is what drives you. It will keep you at the job for long hours and sometimes make you neglect even the most important things in your life, like sleep. When the passion is real, it's almost like a disease. It has driven people from other people, separated families, and even caused people to be homeless. A thin line has to be drawn when dealing with the likes of passion, because it can be as powerful as King Arthur's Excalibur. And though it is manifested on the inside, it must be extinguished on the outside.

When working with children, relationships are the most important part of the job. Kids can tell when you like what you do—they may not pinpoint how they know or even say to you anything they notice, but their actions and how they respond to the things you ask of them will show. It's like a mirror just for you. Your emotions toward your job are translated through their actions.

It is easy for the students to know when you have real passion, and you will know when they are making changes in their daily lives.

There is a phrase I use with other teachers and myself, "Your passion is showing!" In the after-school program one day, a kid showed me that my passion was showing. I had asked the children to read one day and as they were reading, a kid kept coming to the door, looking in and playing around the window. Lo and behold, it was a kid that was supposed to be in our classroom, and he happened to be out or skipping. I went out to him and asked what he was doing outside and not in the classroom, but while I was talking, other kids were there, watching and attempting to distract me from getting on to him. Before I could say anything, the kid I was getting on to told the other kids to leave because, and I quote, "Mr. D. C. does not play."

When these words left his mouth, I was astonished. It was so much to my surprise that he would say something of that nature about me that, for a moment, I was speechless. We then talked about why he was not in the classroom, and when he told me what I believed to be the truth, we went on our ways.

There are many adjectives that kids say about me behind my back and also in front of me, but *mean* is not one of them. As I said, passion could easily be mistaken for anger if you don't have control of it. I know when to be stern about things and when to be relaxed about things, and that is a part of my passion. The children know that I am only there for their best interest and not mine alone, and that is something they need to see more often.

How often is it that a child gets to see what passion looks like coming out of another human being? Passion is extremely rare in our society today. Most people are doing something they feel like they have to do and not something they want to do, and this will affect their outlook on life and their general attitude. If we took a poll and asked the kids if their parents are happy or not so happy about their current jobs, you could probably bet over half of their parents are not so happy with their jobs.

What does it do to a child when they don't understand what it means to have passion, yet people are constantly asking them to tell them what they are passionate about? If I were the child being asked that question, I would immediately ask the adult to answer that question first. Nowadays, passion is being translated to dollar signs, and the more money the job makes, the more passion you will have for it—or at least that is what they are thinking.

Benjamin Franklin once said that anyone that is willing to trade freedom for more security does not deserve either one. And now I say to you, "Anyone who is trading *passion* for security does not deserve either one."

Passion will go beyond monetary value because there is no amount of money you can pay someone for something they are willing to do for free. People are always searching, but hardly finding the thing they love to do the most. When you're good at something, it makes you feel good on the inside. You don't even have to be doing it for you to feel as if you are on top of the world. Many of us settle for just being good at something, no one ever going deeper to see if there is anything they can expand on.

Being good at something is where we start, but not where we are to finish.

People have stayed at jobs because they were very good at the job they were doing, so they assumed that was the job they were made to do. I'll tell you, as I tell everyone else in my life—be careful what you find yourself being good at because it could be the very thing you spend your life on.

Most of you teachers are good at teaching, too. You make it to work on time, you're always in a good mood, and you are constantly making good relationships with the kids you work with. From the outside, it looks like you were made to be a teacher.

How do you know? You might not be feeling it on the inside—there may be something else you were made to do, but you are settling with being a teacher because it is the easiest and you feel as if you know it so well. For those of you who I have just described, this is doing a disservice to not only you, but also the students you have been given in your classroom.

There is a difference between being good at something and being passionate about something. When a person is good at something, they continue to do the thing for their sake; it pays the bills, and they are proud because they are not so bad at it.

On the contrary, passion is different. When you have passion, it is no longer for you to keep the thing you are passionate about on the inside—now the very thing you are passionate about has to be given to the world. The only thing that will make you feel worthy of the passion you have been given is how you use it for the sake of others. Most people spend their entire life trying to find the purpose that serves them best, but your purpose was always meant to serve others.

So, it is in your serving of others that you will discover your purpose.

Passion is often cultivated through acts of service. Humans, being social creatures by nature, we often get caught up in serving on multiple fronts. Home, job, church, community, etc., but each one of these particular services are also a part of our social well-being or connected to some form of social groups or gatherings. As a result, we become passionate about the things we do religiously. This is by no means a bad thing, but true passion will lead to a better product! What I am suggesting here is that we dive intuitively into ourselves and really find out what we are so good at that it doesn't feel like work and you don't need others to motivate you to do it or hold you accountable to be consistent. Real change and great services are the by-product of true passion for the work.

Ralph Waldo Emerson quoted the value of good work:

> *If a man can write a better book, preach a better sermon or make a better mouse trap than his neighbors, though he builds his house in the woods, the world will make a beaten path to his door.*

We live in a world constantly in need of people with passion, and every day, they are born. It's like a seed: the power and the potential of a seed is always in the seed, but cultivation is still needed. These powers in you have to be noticed by you and you alone first. Only then will you know where it is needed the most. In other words, "get into it" and live within it! Find what your passion is and live in that space using that power, only getting stronger by the day.

Having passion is like having a superpower, but you have to be in a place where your power is needed. If you are in a place and you seem as useful as everyone else on the job, then that is not where you will find your passion. Your passion will set you apart from everyone else there. You will not be compared to others and they will seek you out for the very thing that you have, the keeper of the knowledge that they need the most.

If you have not discovered your passion yet, that's okay, but you have to keep searching. Kids need to see as many superheroes as they can because this is what will make them feel safe.

When I was a kid, I met a few people in my life that had real passion, and I was young enough to follow behind them for a while. The way it shaped my life was amazing. Seeing a human be great at something was like watching an angel fly untouched by the world.

A big thanks goes out to all the people who inspired me with their passion. I don't know what I would have become if I wasn't able to see it firsthand. My most recent encounter with a passionate person left me with this advice: *What you do will not matter unless you are doing it for someone other than yourself.* It makes no difference how good you are at speaking, unless you are speaking to the masses; it makes no difference how good you are at painting, unless you are painting for someone else to see. And most of all, it does not matter how good you are at teaching, unless you are in a school teaching a child.

Questions for Self-Reflection

1. Are you passionate about teaching?

2. Do the children know you care? If so, how?

3. Would you consider yourself to be good at teaching? If so, how do you know?

4. Do you believe you were made to teach? Explain your answer.

Smart

Smart is when you have knowledge or show signs of quick-witted intelligence.

Kids are not in need of someone who is just as smart as they are; they need someone who knows a lot more than they do. They also are not in need of someone who sees the world as they do, indulging in some of the things they are interested in. Teachers and students should not receive their news from the same outlet. There is no need for a teacher to see the world the same as the students do. Kids need to have the opportunity to talk to someone about new ideas, which leads to an exploration of a new frontier, fostering knowledge and curiosity all at the same time.

We are faced with a world where everyone can receive knowledge without even trying to learn anything. With the internet and the television, you can be just as smart, or smarter, than anyone else, just depends on how long and how much you keep up with. It's not even about if you can retain the right information or not; you just have to say it at the right time of conversation. Heck, because you don't have to be smart at all, you just need to *look* smart.

Misinformation is the main ingredient to social media, big headlines that incorporate no truth, and articles being written with no quantifiable data or statistics. But this is no matter—we are seeking entertainment, not knowledge. What a misfortune it is to be misinformed and run with a seed that is not capable of producing any real fruit.

Teachers and students alike are falling for the same information. How someone learned something is more important than what they learned.

We have come to a place where we are going to have to redefine knowledge. We can no longer say a person is smart just because they have a mouth and vibrations are coming out of it, making sounds that you were not able to make. There was a time when you had to look up things in places so specific, there was no telling where you'd have to go and what you would learn in the process of it all. Dictionaries, encyclopedias, and just books, books, and more books were your only hope if you were going to learn something new. Not just read something new, but learn something, know it like the back of your hand, and have confidence in your information because you took the time to read it. Learning is something we have to be taught how to do; we have to know what it feels like to retain information and also use it.

Being smart is not all that it used to be. It used to be an honor to be known to your community as a smart individual, and that would last a lifetime. Now you can be as smart as Einstein today and as thoughtless as a caveman tomorrow. You do not have to know much to be smarter than the kids you are working with, but you do have to be living a different life than them.

Being smart does not mean going against everything they say all of the time. It just means because you are the teacher and they are the student, everything you say and do helps them learn, and as a teacher, you need to be constantly working on getting smarter.

If you are the type of person that has no clue how to get smarter for the sake of your students, reading is a good place to start. There are so many things that come out of looking for information in this way, and so many people's lives were changed just from setting time aside to read. Abraham Lincoln, the sixteenth president of the United States of America, was a product of self-education. The late president's family could not afford to send him to a school, so he received lots of books and immersed himself in them. This became most of his education. He read everything he could get his hands on, and by doing so, he became the president of the United States.

Reading for knowledge is a lost art. People *are* reading, but no one is reading because they desperately *want* to learn about something new. People read what they have to and not because they want to. Having the time to read is a factor, but when it comes to learning anything, you have to make time—nothing learns itself. And if you are going to be working with children, you have to know what it feels like to work hard on your intelligence so you can communicate the stress of it to them; you can be familiar.

So when it comes to knowledge, what is it that is going to be able to separate one from the other? Not much, and that is very sad to say. People are mostly on the same level when it comes to knowledge, and knowing something to a T is not needed anymore. We declare someone smarter than the other by their degree. No one has to prove their intellect anymore; it is solely based on where you went to college and what degree you received while you were there.

The saddest thing about this is that so many people are not only cheating their way to get into college, but they are also cheating their way to get out of college. Their degree won't say what their GPA was; it will only say what they went to get and did they receive it with honors or not. And when it comes to teaching students, they are now saying that a degree in education is almost as easy as a degree in criminal justice.

So, with all of this, where does it leave the students that we leave with our teachers? In a class where they have an instructor that did not have to prove themselves to get the job they received.

Kids are constantly being placed in classrooms with a teacher that does not know much more than their students. Teachers want to be cool, and hip, and in the know when it comes to popular things on social media, and this will have a bad effect on the students. As I said before, teachers cannot be involved in the same things as their students.

So, as an educator I would strongly advise not spending so much time on social media as possible, to the point of not even needing it anymore. For me this worked wonders. When I deleted all social-media platforms, it was like breathing for the first time. I had so much time and way less distractions; I was reading, painting, and learning a different language. Not only was I beginning to feel smarter, I was actually getting smarter. My retention and my focus were expanding. Not spending so much time on useless stuff was working to my benefit.

As an educator what you do in your spare time will matter the most—it will be what makes you or breaks you. When I decided to use my phone less, this was just the first step of me managing my time better. There are so many ways we can be more productive, and when you realize and feel the difference, you might even be forever changed.

This is the target that we are trying to get our students to realize. The only way they are going to make a change in their life is you first have to make a change in yours. Show them what a smart individual looks like, show them that you are more than just a degree, and you will make them change just by your actions. Show them how to plan ahead so they have more control over the outcome. When they see you planning, they, too, might start.

We have to be the change we want to see in them or else how are we ever going to notice when things actually start to change? Don't just look smart—be smart.

QUESTIONS FOR SELF-REFLECTION

1. Are people as smart as they used to be in your personal opinion? Explain you answer.

2. What is more important, how you learned something or what you learned?

3. What could you do to become more smart/ productive?

4. Why is it that you have not deleted your social media, or what is keeping you from doing so?

ROLE MODEL

A **role model** is a person looked at by others as an example to be imitated.

One thing I always ask myself is two questions: If someone was watching me, what would I want them to see, and if the entire world was planning on following my example, would I be pleased to see what becomes of the world?

Well, there are people watching me every day, and if you are an educator and don't consider yourself a role model by now, you have a huge problem. There are so many things as a teacher you have to keep up with in order to be a good role model for students. At times, it's overwhelming, you might literally have to be as clean as a politician to be a teacher. The students should be able to model your behavior and make the entire world a better place.

I have my own personal list of things I like to keep in mind when working around kids, one of which is dressing nice and neat. I wake up and iron my clothes most of the time, when they are needed. Not only does it make me feel confident, but approachable. Because we are social creatures, we look for these little things in people and we try to fit our social life around their standards. This means one day kids might decide to dress just like you, and it will be because of you how they look in the end. So, I take dressing very seriously. The kids may not have parents that are able to buy or even afford some of the things I wear, but that does not stop me from wearing them.

When I was a kid, my mom and grandmother bought all of my clothes, and they were nothing like what I wear now. I was very appreciative to have the things I had growing up, but most of the people I looked up to wore nothing like the clothes that were purchased for me. They were dressing me like the people they thought looked nice.

Why? Because this is just what we do as humans. Fashion is based around who they can get to wear their clothing to influence society. The fashion industry knows that if they can score the biggest celebrity to wear something from their brand, the sky is the limit on how much can be made. So, they spend most of their investing money on finding the right celebrity.

Now you may not be a celebrity, but you are what the kids are going to be seeing every day and if you make enough of an impact in their lives, they will gladly dress like you when they get older. I'm not giving anyone permission to judge what they wear, because it's all objective at the end of the day. I'm just letting you know that this is one way I do my part to try and influence the youth of today. And you may not consider yourself that great of a dresser, but if your clothes are cleaned and pressed most of the time, this is good enough for them to take with them the rest of their lives.

One other thing when it comes to physical appearance is being well-groomed, and as I said before, these things are objective. Coming in with neat hair and a clean face and you smell nice is big. Some kids do not get to see this modeled in the home for reasons we do not know.

I was lucky enough to grow up with a lot of women in my life, and being the only male, I walked a tightrope. If I ever went around them not smelling very good, they would bring it up, and that was never a good feeling. I consider smelling nice to just be a way of showing others your consideration of the shared air space.

A good role model should always practice being kind to others, showing mercy and forgiveness in every situation. Kids are not very good at being kind to each other and they very much need to see an example of what it means to be nice.

I do get snappy with the students I'm working with too often. For one, there is no reason for me to be taking anything they say or do personally, and for two, because they need to see how it feels for someone to forgive them for something they might have done to intentionally hurt you. This is not going to be easy for anyone working with children—I was spit on many times and had to let it go. It wasn't worth losing my job or their respect, because when you act out of character, you lose their respect.

When I am kind, I am thoughtful. I may do it by sharing candy with them for nothing, or I may talk to them for no good reason about nothing that really matters. I try to be unintentional to them, but it's very intentional to me when I am being kind to them. At that given moment, I am showing them what it looks like so they can model that behavior. And I am always cheerful when I am approaching them.

This is also something they may not get to see modeled at their home. Their parents may not be kind for many different reasons, but no matter the reasons, if they are not able to see it in their first home, at least they can see it in their second home, and that is where school comes in. Some of your students may not be emotionally stable, and that may be directly from the home, but you have to be emotionally stable for their sake and for the possibility of them noticing and believing they can do the same thing.

Everyone wants to know that someone thinks their behavior is worth following, but we should never want this for needs of validation. I used to want to know that someone was watching me, and I would want to be rewarded for such good behavior. But then I realized that this was the exact behavior that I hated when the kids did it. All day, kids are constantly looking for ways to impress you, but not because they want you to be proud. It is usually because they are looking to gain something out of the whole deal. You need to live a life worth following so they can model your style and actions. If you are insincere with your behaviors, they will be also in the same ways.

In order for people to feel you are worth following, you have to model the same behavior constantly until they know this is who you are. A lot of teachers do a good job of doing this at the beginning of the year, but by Christmas they are worn out. Kids are going to challenge you when it comes to being true to yourself, because once you decide this is who you are going to be, it will be like baptism by fire. Kids are either going to bring the worst out of you or the absolute best.

The most important thing we should model is being proactive and not reactive. What I have learned with pleasure in these short years of my life is the best way to respond to anything is by being proactive. I look out into this world, and what I see people teaching children is very dangerous for our society. The one thing I would like to model to the best of my abilities is to react as if I was always thinking about the outcome.

When I was in my beginning stages of learning how to play chess, the fellow I played with was amazing. I could never win games. He would constantly bully me the entire time during the game. Most of the time I would be doing great, but somehow he always had a plan that would usually win the game for him. We are still playing to this day, and I've beaten him many times. But the one thing that I have not been able to grasp is how to control my emotional reactions to the things he does on the board. Every time he takes one of my pieces that I did not anticipate, my emotions make me desire payback, and that is when I begin to lose the game. There is a quote that reads, "Think like a [person] of action, act like a [person] of thought."

This is the most important lesson that we should be cultivating in our youth and the students that we come into contact with. They are not able to act before they think, so this behavior I try to model for them. I do it by making sure that every action that I have provokes thought in them.

Let's say one kid hits another, and neither of them get into really big trouble. This is questionable to the classroom, and either we are going to have way more fights happen than we need or none at all.

My reaction in chess had to be unpredictable for me to have a fighting chance against the guy I played chess with, and so does our reaction to our students.

For the most part, there are many ways to become a bad role model for your students, but there are also just as many ways to be a good one. You have to take a look at yourself and figure out what it is that you should change about you for the sake of these kids and our society. What we fail to realize is that all kids are looking for the next best thing to follow, and that should be our number-one goal.

We should go head to head with the world and demand that our kids follow our behaviors and not anyone else's. We are allowing so many other things to raise the youth for us, and it's not doing a good job at all. We need to be their only role model, and we need to do whatever it takes to keep it that way.

These kids need us now more than ever, and we are going to have to step up to the plate.

Questions for Self-Reflection

1. Would you consider yourself a good role model? Explain your answer.

2. Do you take pride in what you wear?

3. What makes you a good role model?

4. Are you emotionally stable enough to work with children?

5. Are your behaviors sincere at all times? Explain your answer.

___

___

___

___

___

LOVE

Love is feeling or showing love or great care.

Love is defined in so many ways in today's instant-gratification society. Social media has shaped the way we see everything, and love is the last frontier that it is taking over like a wildfire. Love is supposed to be unconditional, and when it is real, change and progress can be made. However, no one currently knows what unconditional love looks like anymore, so we do not notice when we are receiving it.

Our students are suffering the most and not getting anything out of life, not even the love that they so desperately need.

Love first is supposed to come from a child's home, and when it does and is done right, that child has no problem loving others. It seems to me that children are born with a very big heart from the start, so unconditional as they move around their space.

Have you ever noticed one of your students coming from a bad situation and not noticing that their situation is bad at all? A kid could literally not be eating every night and not even show their parents any type of hate or blame—if anything, it motivates them to do whatever they can to help their parents out, even if it means forfeiting their dreams and goals. Kids love whatever they have and whatever they are shown, and until someone comes along and shows them differently, they will always see love the way it's been taught to them.

That energy that kids pose toward their parents is what we need to be trying to gain in the classroom. We need kids to love our schools so much that they are willing to give up anything for us and do whatever they have to do to make us proud. Pulling out that same passion and love they have for their parents is not going to happen, though it may seem like it could. We would first have to have true, unconditional love for them. Only a parent has the ability to really show this without trying. We, on the other hand, have to try really, really hard to do this.

During that time that we are trying to prove that we really love and care about the students we work with, we are also losing so much ground. Our love just doesn't look as real as their parents does, and it's because we just can't love them that much. Because, at the end of a school day, we get to go home, and so do they. If someone even asked you if you could stay extra time in an attempt to prove your love, would any one of us as educators even be willing?

So often we start out on the wrong foot with the children that we end up loving the most. What I'm currently learning about a student that I have is that the more I choose to love him through all of his bad behavior—spitting, hitting, and destroying property—the more I can love him the next day and the next day. My love will only grow the more I forgive, and now it almost doesn't matter what the kid does; I have so much love for him, I'm unaffected by his actions.

Getting to this point was hard to do because so often I had to tell myself that this was not about me. I needed to love him as much as I could. I'm not going to lie, it was difficult. Some days I'd laugh a lot, but you know what they say—if you don't laugh, you are definitely going to cry. You have to push through these situations because the homes they come from may not be showing them good love. The attention that they receive at home may be negative attention, and this is where the problem is. That is why it's so important that we show them positive energy.

What may look like a bad situation at home and a lack of love may not be the same from a child's point of view. Although the view of a child is simple and narrow, doesn't mean that seeds cannot be planted. A simple and narrow ground is perfect soil for a seed to take root.

Every kid wants the same thing at heart throughout their childhood. And what is that, you might ask? Attention! Some may often gain it from the wrong places, and some may gain it from better ones. But the students that we are always having trouble with are not getting it at all; they are getting negative attention and they are settling for it because negative attention is better than no attention at all. And this is the love that we will be able to give them unconditionally, because love in our classroom can be defined as positive reinforcement.

Because we do not get to go home with the students, we don't know what happens when they get there. We are not able to love them from a distance, though it is possible our students are not mature enough to know when they are receiving love from a distance. We have to give them so much positivity during a school day that they crave it and begin a desire to have it more often.

This is how you build an appetite. It is in no way our jobs to redefine what love looks like for them, and if that is what you are thinking, stop now, because those are shoes you cannot fill without a lot of work. Just be there for them every time they are showing enough good behavior for positive energy.

So, love in the classroom is different. How? because it's simple things that lead to rewarding outcomes. As a teacher, I always try to carry the heavy load as much as possible. I heard a pastor say when he was young, his older brother and him would have to carry a pail of water up a hill to the house after going down to the well to get it. He continued that one day they got smart and used a stick in the handles of the bucket to have more leverage, and although the stick made for a great idea, there was still going to be two ends. Because his brother was the oldest, he always carried the short end of the stick and gave his little brother the longer end so that it would be easier for him to carry it up the hill.

Our students are always in need of help, and we can show them love by giving them the longer end of the stick. They are learning something for the first time, and we have to keep that in mind. No matter how tough and strong we want them to be, we need to give them the easier side of the work if that's what it takes.

How many of us as educators even love them enough to be remotely interested in their lives? Asking something as simple as "How is your day going?" means the world to them. They may not always tell you, but it does. Imagine what it would feel like if you were having a bad day and finally someone came up to you and asked if you needed to talk with someone. How might that feel? I'll tell you what it would feel like—it would feel like you were loved, and something that simple can make the biggest impact.

Doing this little thing becomes normal after a while, but that is not the goal. The goal is for it to be sincere and right on time when asked. Doing things for the sake of doing it is not translated as love to anyone.

However, on the flip side, when negative attention is being shown to them, it shows up very easy. There are many children who find it easier to express hate instead of love. The reason being is that it's all they know how to show; that is what is being shown to them on a daily basis. When they go home, some of them may not go home to a loving environment, and when they come to school, majority of the time it is a very hostile environment due to the other students alone. Their days are in turmoil from the moment they wake up, and the only question left to ask is which part of their day do you want to be? Do you want to add to all the current noise in their life, or do you want to be the breath of fresh air? They deserve a break at some point, but who is going to give that break to them if not you?

Be giving, be real, be open to things they like—these are some of the ways you are going to be able to push out all that bad energy. As educators, we seem to be very good at making sure that all the things that are bad are not happening in our classroom, but we are leaving a void when we rid them of those bad behaviors. And what happens sooner or later? Those things come back into to play.

An old Cherokee is teaching his grandson about life. "A fight is going on inside me," he said to the boy. "It is a terrible fight and it is between two wolves. One is evil—he is anger, envy, sorrow, regret, greed, arrogance, self-pity, guilt, resentment, inferiority, lies, false pride, superiority, and ego."

He continued, "The other is good—he is joy, peace, love, hope, serenity, humility, kindness, benevolence, empathy, generosity, truth, compassion, and faith. The same fight is going on inside of you—and inside every other person, too."

The grandson thought about it for a minute and then asked his grandfather, "Which wolf will win?"

The old Cherokee simply replied, "The one you feed."

When working with children, that is all we are dealing with for the most part—emotional wolves that need to be fed. The one being fed is going to triumph over the other, but you have to fill that space that is left behind. When the bad begins to go out, reinforce the area with the good so there is no space for it to return. Misbehaving and doing things for no apparent reason has to become unfamiliar to them, and when it does, only then might it be gone for good.

It's hard to love anything without some sort of benefit coming with it in the current times that we live in. There is so much being offered, and so fast, that we don't have time to choose which path is right for us. But just because we may not have a clue on what it feels like to receive unconditional love, does not mean that we don't know how to give it. This is a natural feeling; it is more natural than hate or any other feeling. It is so familiar that, for a while, we don't even have to try at times; it just comes out.

The first emotion we have ever felt was unconditional love. This is how it was when we were born. Into the arms of a stranger, and for no apparent reason they loved us and cared for us, and when we're old enough to understand, we called them mother.

This love had such a huge effect on us that it carried us through most of our youth, and we tried to give this same type of love to others and everything there was. Our mother fed us, bathed us, and watched everything we did for a while to make sure we were not going to get into anything that might hurt us. When she would leave us, she would make sure she found the best person possible to take care of us while she was gone.

This would go on for years.

She would also call us sweet names and celebrate our every achievement, and this became addicting. We got to the point where we wanted to give something back to this person that was taking such good care of us. The times when we were happy, it made her happy, and when we were sad, it made her sad. As we got older, the only thing we could do is realize that by being us, we were giving back to her.

As we got older, we learned about the world, and there was so much we wanted to do and so many people we wanted to meet that sooner or later, she knew we would abandon her. When that day finally came, she was heartbroken, but not in an angry way, just in a way that would miss us.

The entire time, we were nothing but work for her. Because of us, she had to have two jobs and sacrifice things she might have wanted to do for fun, and she gave all of that up just to take care of us for a while. The thought never even crossed our minds about leaving or not; we are sure that leaving is the best thing to do, so we leave.

We go out into the world hoping to find all that we want in it and maybe some of that love our mothers gave us, but we don't. And when we don't, for a while we are angry about it and we even get a little selfish. And just in the nick of time, someone comes along and teaches us how to love again.

We were loved unconditionally first. That is why it is such an easy emotion to learn how to do again. Some of you are mothers and fathers, so it should come very easily to you. For those of you who are not a parent, think about your parents or the people that raised you. Mimic that behavior.

These kids need so much love, it's hardly even possible to fill the void that has been placed in them. But it is our job to do it, and that is the reason we took this job in the first place—not to just be in a school all day, but to make a difference. Love is the only way we are going to change the world one child at a time.

Unconditional does not mean *unrealistic*. Both parties, at some point, have to be giving it simultaneously so you don't feel like a complete failure. A working partnership between a child and adult may not always share unconditional love, but most often than not it will be because of the adult and not the child. It's crazy because the one most capable of change is the one most often not changing. As an educator, you are the dog with the most experience, and on top of that, you are the one being fed.

Adults need to love exactly as children do!

Questions for Self-Reflection

1. Where does a kid first learn how to love or see what love is? How can you attempt to mimic this love?

____
____
____
____
____

2. Have you ever loved a student like your own child?

____
____
____
____
____

3. Do you intentionally show interest in your student? If so, how?

____
____
____
____
____

4. How might you practice pushing the bad energy out of your students?

____
____
____
____
____

ACKNOWLEDGMENTS

During the three years of writing this book, I had the privilege of meeting so many people and working with many students. The inspiration that I was able to gain and the knowledge could have only been learned in the spaces I was welcomed in.

First and foremost, I would like to thank my mom and dad, who raised me in a two-parent household that gave me the freedom to dream. Secondly, my wonderful grandparents that always showed me love, and my sisters and cousins that continue to motivate me to this day.

This book is very special to me, but I would have never been able to write it without Susan Rutherford, Sam and Vivian Neeley Jr., Lisa Sanger, Mr. Carter, John and Karen Wright, Arthur Coardes, Anthony Jeremiah Nash, Jeffery McPherson, Martin Hilbert, Gerald Byrd, Hammad Ghulam-Hussain, Robert Anthony, Deandre Dukes, Martez Farris, Ronald Albert Taylor Jr., Mr. Shaq, George Thomasson III, Damontae Henderson, Dee Banks, Jeffrey Anderson, and Edymar Salazar Fernandez. These are the people that kept me consistent in my pursuit of my vision. These were the people that had my back and kept me going during this entire process, and though this book was completed in three years, it was ten years in the making.

CPSIA information can be obtained
at www.ICGtesting.com
Printed in the USA
LVHW102028220622
721764LV00008BA/854